Berlitz®
Marrakesh

Front cover: colourful yarns in the souk

Right: Gnaoua musicians on Jemaa el-Fna

TOP 10 ATTRACTIONS

Koutoubia Mosque •
Visible from almost everywhere in the city, the 12th-century minaret is one of Marrakesh's oldest and most distinct monuments *(page 30)*

Jemaa el-Fna • At dusk this becomes one of the world liveliest squares, with food stalls and a host of performe *(page 26)*

Essaouira • With its port, markets and beautifu medina, this makes a delightful excursion *(page*

The Souks • Colourful, noisy, exotic, exhaustin tempting, crowded, chaotic – a full blow to all t senses *(page 32)*

dersa Ben Youssef • The beautifully decorated 16th-century ranic school is open to non-Muslims *(page 38)*

Ourika Valley • When the buzz of the medina becomes too much, head for this quiet and beautiful valley *(page 68)*

éliz • Colonial hitecture, shopping and ne of Morocco's most citing nightlife *(page 56)*

Majorelle Garden • The contrasting electric blue walls make the green of French painter Jacques Majorelle's exotic garden look all the greener *(page 63)*

dian Tombs • The 66 al tombs are notable for ir lavish Andalusian-style coration *(page 46)*

El-Badi Palace • It took an army of craftsmen more than 25 years to finish Ahmed el-Mansour's splendid palace *(page 49)*

CONTENTS

60

102

40

INTRODUCTION

From being one of the sleepiest places in North Africa, Marrakesh has emerged in recent years as one of its liveliest and most welcoming cities. Yet although the crowds are new, the reasons for its appeal are not. With its mix of Berber and Arab charm, its dusty alleys, its plain doorways opening to reveal opulent courtyards, its bright light and rich colours, Marrakesh has always been a place of fascination.

Even if you don't get through those doorways, Marrakesh still has plenty to offer visitors: the remains of its 16th- and 17th-century glory days, some imposing early 20th-century buildings, beautiful gardens and the ever-busy souks are more than enough reasons to visit. There are more attractions still on the way: the horizon is now dotted with cranes, busy developing the city into the epicentre of an ambitious plan that will transform Moroccan tourism.

Location, Location, Location

Marrakesh owes its existence, its character and its new-found success to its location. Sitting at the northern feet of the Atlas Mountains and at the southern end of the lush Moroccan plains, it came into being as a market town where mountain Berbers and Arabs from the plains came to trade with the trans-Saharan caravan merchants.

The city's souks were packed with ivory, senna, ebony and slaves from beyond the Sahara, rugs and jewellery from the mountains and glass, spun cottons, teapots and weapons from the north. Since then Marrakesh has been an imperial capital; the hated rival of Meknes and Fez, which lie further north; the city the colonial French never managed to subdue;

The medina walls

and later a hangout for hippies. It is now one of the most enjoyable and exotic short-haul escape destinations from nearby Europe.

The new tourist developments play to one of the city's strengths: its climate. Although the high summers can be blisteringly hot, winters are usually mild and often sunny, spring and autumn invariably blissful. Add to that the exoticism of the souks and the lure of the nearby snow-capped mountains, visible from medina rooftops, and it is easy to see why so many people are enchanted by Marrakesh. The city is home to well over one million people, but unofficially the number is thought to be closer to two million, one third of whom are members of several Berber tribes originally from the Rif and Atlas mountains.

Yet as well as a playground for foreign visitors, Marrakesh remains a vibrant Moroccan city and one that punches above its weight. It may no longer be the capital – Rabat on the Atlantic coast has that honour – but for a long time it has been the country's most famous city. Eighteenth- and early 19th-century Europeans called the city and the country by the same name, just as they did Algiers and Algeria, Tunis and Tunisia: in many ways, Marrakesh remains synonymous with Morocco.

The Heart of the Matter

The city is divided into several distinct districts, the best-known being the old city inside the walls, which is known as the medina and dates from 1070. Until little more than a century ago the miles of rust-red mudbrick walls enclosed the entire city. Behind the series of gates, some of them seemingly straight out of fairy tales, lies a town sub-divided by interior walls and gates into distinct districts: one for the royal palaces, one – the Mellah – for the Jews, one for the souks and so on.

Rahba Kedima – the Spice Square

The medina remains the main attraction. It is a place where narrow, winding alleys unite communities around the pillars of the mosque, the school, the baker, the hammam and the clusters of courtyard houses known as *riads*. The medina has no large hotels (with the sole exception of the world-famous Mamounia, built just inside the Bab Jdid, the New Gate), but what it does have are more than 500 *riads* converted and available to rent, by the room or in their entirety, by visitors.

In spite of the influx of visitors, the medina has retained much of the character and interest that led to it being inscribed on Unesco's World Heritage list in 1985. In particular, it has preserved its unique centrepiece: the Jemaa el-Fna, a triangular space beside the souks. By day, 'La Place', as it is known locally, serves nothing more exciting than juice from Souss oranges and a few herbal medicines. At night, however, it is completely transformed. Part of the space is devoted to food stands, where foreigners rub shoulders with local people to sample couscous, fish, sheep's head, snails and a long list of other local delicacies. The rest is taken up by entertainers, among them sufi musicians, magicians, snake-charmers, story-tellers and many others who fancy their chances of attracting a ring of spectators around them.

New Town Marrakesh

The French were the first to build seriously outside the walls, beginning soon after 1912 when Morocco was colonised. Their Ville Nouvelle, which takes its name, Guéliz, from a small hill nearby, was laid out as a suburb of broad leafy avenues and large detached houses. It remains distinct from the medina, although it is no longer as sedate as it once was (the exception being the garden area known

Bougainvillea on blue at the Majorelle Garden

as Hivernage, which still has some fabulous early 20th-century villas). Other parts of Guéliz, particularly around the central artery of Avenue Mohammed V, are super-swanky, the place to find the city's most elegant boutiques, bars and restaurants. Here, too, is one of Marrakesh's most popular sights, the house and garden created in the 1920s by French painter Jacques Majorelle, who brilliantly combined local greens with a shade of cobalt paint now known as Majorelle blue. Twenty years ago you would have been laughed at for wanting to live in the Palmeraie. But the area of palm groves beyond the French-built new town has now become home to some of the city's wealthiest residents and some of its most beautiful hotels. A road snakes through the palm groves off the main Marrakesh–Fez road, and the Palmeraie circuit, although no longer as calm as it once was, still runs through an area of great beauty.

> **Garden city**
>
> From its foundation, Marrakesh was a city of gardens. A growing population has meant that there are now few public green spaces inside the medina, but many *riads* have fig, palm or orange trees in their courtyards. Marrakesh beyond the walls is still very green in places such as Hivernage, the Palmeraie and the Agdal and Majorelle Gardens.

The Marrakesh Brand

It had been coming for a few years, but when the Moroccan government paved the way for budget flights from Europe and international-brand clubs opened their doors, it was clear that Marrakesh had arrived as a key destination on the global party circuit. Following on from Ibiza and St Tropez, it has reinvented itself as the playground for wealthy Europeans, where billionaires and the slightly less well-off come to have fun.

King Mohammed VI has played a key role in recreating Marrakesh, making it the centrepiece of an ambitious plan to increase tourism revenue. This has involved more than opening the skies to numerous airlines and promoting nightclubs and new hotels. Marrakesh now also has beautifully restored public buildings, a lively arts and cultural scene and a growing market for upscale products, many of which find their way into Western luxury stores. The Marrakesh Film Festival grows in stature each year and the fledgling literary, art and music festivals have begun to attract attention. All this provides entertainment for visitors who want even more than stunning landscapes, extraordinary architecture, a wonderful climate and a welcome that goes far beyond a glass of sweet mint tea.

A restored *riad*

Out of Town

Many visitors who choose to stay in *riads* in the medina find themselves looking for distraction beyond the confines of the city's red walls. Happily, it is easy to get out of town and there are plenty of entertainments nearby, from large, luxurious swimming pools to country club-style retreats tucked away in rose gardens. All this, and the glory of the High Atlas mountains just a short drive away, makes Marrakesh the perfect place for a holiday packed with contrasts.

A BRIEF HISTORY

Marrakesh began as an outpost of a Saharan kingdom, became the capital of an empire that stretched up to the Pyrenees, and was ruled over by one of the most colourful and extraordinary peoples in the long history of Morocco. Its value lay in its location, on the crossroads of trans-Saharan trade routes linking mountain and plain, desert and coast.

The city's history is not short of incident, nor of romance, bloodshed and brilliance. It seems to seep through every wall of every alley and hang over every tea-punctuated conversation.

Morocco's Dynasties

Marrakesh owes its unique character to its history. Although it sits on the northern side of the great barrier of the Atlas Mountains, it was created by people from the south. The Almoravids, a confederation of Berber tribes from the Sahara, were inspired and united by Ibn Yassin, a holy man from the Souss Valley (southeast of today's Agadir), who preached a pure form of Islam. With him they declared a *jihad* (holy war) against the influence of the Andalucian Moors, who allowed alcohol to be drunk and men to take more than four wives. Their zeal carried

Berber village in the
Atlas Mountains

Master builder

Ali ben Youssef was one of the great early builders: in what is now Algeria he created the mosque of Tlemcen and in Fez he built the central Karaouine Mosque. In his capital, Marrakesh, he built the mosque and medersa that bears his name. The carving in all the monuments was done by masters brought over from Andalucia.

them to victory beyond the Atlas, where, around 1070, they founded Marrakesh.

Marrakesh was originally the Almoravids' northern-most settlement, which they surrounded with *pisé* (adobe) walls. But the Almoravid leader, Youssef ben Tachfine, had ambitions in the north. In 1075 he conquered the central city of Fez and within five years, he had control over most of what is now Morocco, effectively creating the first Moroccan state. Before the 11th century, the country we know as Morocco was divided into many different tribal territories, Arab city-states and contested trade routes.

Youssef ben Tachfine didn't stop there. Ten years later he crossed the straits to Spain, where the Catholics were claiming victories over the Andalucian Muslim princes. He was successful there too, and his son Ali ben Youssef, who succeeded him in 1107, inherited an empire that stretched from West Africa to the Pyrenees, from the Atlantic to Algeria. The Almoravids brought with them the technology necessary for surviving in the desert. In Marrakesh, they built *khettara*, underground irrigation channels, to supply their new city with water from the Atlas Mountains.

The Almohad Princes

The Almoravids over-extended themselves, but it is more likely that the dynasty fell because their reformist zeal began to wane. In their place rose another reformist Berber dynasty, not from the Sahara, but from the Atlas Mountains, inspired by a

Towers such as the minaret of the Kasbah Mosque owe their origin to the great Almohad sultan Yacoub el-Mansour

preacher by the name of Ibn Toumert. Ibn Toumert's targets were obvious: the Almoravids allowed their women to ride horses and had been increasingly corrupted by Andalucian ideas. The movement gathered momentum after the preacher's death thanks to the military genius of his successors, particularly the third Almohad sultan. Yacoub el-Mansour.

Sultan Yacoub earned his title 'el-Mansour', the Victorious, for his exploits in Spain, where he defeated the Christians in 1195. He pushed east as far as Tripoli as well, and for the first time united the Maghreb under a single ruler, based in Marrakesh.

He built across the empire, most notably constructing towers in Rabat (the Tour Hassan), Seville (the Giralda) and Marrakesh (the Koutoubia). The Bab Agnaou (the ornate gate into the Kasbah) is another reminder of the Almohads' austerely beautiful taste in architecture.

Merenid medersa

Although the Merenids chose Fez as their capital, they did build a medersa in Marrakesh, the forerunner of the Medersa Ben Youssef, exanded later by the Saadians.

The dynasty was doomed soon after Yacoub's death. His successor, Mohammed en-Nasr, moved against the Christians in Spain, hoping to push them beyond the Pyrenees. His defeat at Las Navas de Tolosa in 1212 was the start of a rapid decline: in less than half a century, the Almohads lost most of their Spanish territories, including Seville, and were then edged out of Algeria, Fez and eventually Morocco. With them went Marrakesh's prominence: the Merenid dynasty that succeeded them, and which ruled Morocco for three centuries, made Fez their capital.

The Saadians

For more than 500 years, Morocco had been ruled by Berber dynasties who had come from the south. But in the 16th century, as a result of increasing Portuguese control along the Atlantic coast, an Arab family, the Saadians, rose to prominence in the Souss, building a base in Taroudant in the Souss Valley.

The defining moment for the dynasty came in 1578, when the youthful King Sebastian I of Portugal invaded Morocco, in order to support the claim of the deposed Saadian ruler Abu Abdallah Mohammed II against his uncle, Abd Al-Malik Saadi, and thereby reclaim Portugal's coastal bases. The ensuing 'Battle of the Three Kings' at Ksar el-Kebir (near Larache in northern Morocco) ended in the death of all three protagonists and the decisive defeat of Portuguese forces.

The man who benefited from this was Ahmed el-Mansour, who became sultan in 1578. With the ransoms paid to release the Portuguese soldiers captured in battle and with revenues from trade boosted by a stable government, he created an army strong enough to march across the Sahara and take control of Timbuktu, the key to the trade in sub-Saharan gold and slaves.

The Golden One

They called el-Mansour 'ed-Dahabi', the Golden One, and with good reason, for he restored the country and Marrakesh's wealth and standing. Under Sultan Ahmed, the city once more became a glittering centre of patronage. He built a magnificent palace, el-Badi, 'the Incomparable', and its name was no exaggeration: no building in the region came close to it in grandeur. Elsewhere in the city, Ahmed's monuments included the re-built Medersa Ben Youssef and the Saadian Tombs, the compound where he and his dynasty were buried in tombs that match the magnificence of the finest Andalucian work (see page 45).

The entrance to the Saadian Tombs

But like many despots before and since, Ahmed failed to establish a clear successor and on his death in 1603, his descendants fought over the throne, weakening central rule so much that within just a few decades the empire had crumbled.

The Alaouites

As before in Morocco's history, change came like a breath of hot wind from the south. While the Saadians fought among themselves, the Alaouites, a tribe who originated from the oases of the Tafilalet and claimed descent from the Prophet Mohammed, began to unite southern tribes around their base in Rissani, on the edge of the Sahara. It wasn't until 1669, more than half a century after Ahmed's death, that the Alaouite Sultan Moulay Rachid moved on Marrakesh. Rachid held power for just three years before being killed in a palace coup. In contrast, his successor Moulay Ismail ruled for 54 years and laid the foundations of the dynasty that continues to rule Morocco today.

Ismail's heirs were less successful, as his numerous sons (he is said to have fathered more than 1,000 children) disputed the throne for 30 years. Once again power fractured and the kingdom went into a long, slow decline throughout much of the 18th century. Marrakesh went with it. Without

The Cruel Sultan

Moulay Ismail (1672–1727) was one of the more bloodthirsty characters of Moroccan history. With an army of 150,000 African mercenaries he drove the Portuguese out of their Atlantic strongholds, the Ottomans back to the current frontier with Algeria and the English out of Tangier. For Marrakesh and the other imperial city, Fez, his reign was a disaster. Wanting to avoid the glorification of earlier dynasties, Moulay Ismail destroyed all traces of them and set about creating what he hoped would be the greatest of all Moroccan cities, Meknes, 60km (38 miles) from Fez. His palace complex, intended to rival Versailles (and today a Unesco World Heritage Site), was built using materials looted from Saadian palaces. It took Ismail's workers 12 years to strip Marrakesh's el-Badi palace of all its treasures.

stability, the trade routes no longer flourished. When Europeans began looking to North Africa for trade and adventure, they initially avoided Morocco for being too dangerous and difficult to penetrate.

But a succession of sultans exploited foreign interest and for more than a century played the British off against their rivals, the French and Spanish, for a stake in the nation's commerce. While the British concentrated their interests in the trading ports of Essaouira and Tangier, and the Spanish settled along the Atlantic and on the north coast, the French strengthened their hold on neighbouring Algeria, which they had invaded in 1830.

Marrakesh in the early 19th century

French Protectorate

The Moroccan sultans held out against European pressure for more than a century. But in 1912, faced with Berber tribes outside the gates of his capital in Fez and a rival proclaiming his sultanate in nearby Meknes, the ruling sultan Moulay Hafid signed an accord, the Treaty of Fez, that effectively handed over sovereignty to France and made the country a French colony with its capital in Rabat.

Marrakesh had a central role to play in the story of French colonisation. French forces struggled to take control of the

Glaoui's palaces

T'hami el-Glaoui grew immensely wealthy by controlling trade, both legal and illicit, in the High Atlas south of Marrakesh. With some of the proceeds, he built palaces, among them a magnificent Kasbah in the mountains at Telouet and the Dar el-Pasha in Marrakesh.

tribes in the south, where the landscape, climate and the nature of the tribal communities were against them. With the outbreak of World War I, the French did not have the manpower to fight their way through the region. Instead, the French governor General Hubert Lyautey, based in the new capital, Rabat, relied on diplomacy and made a deal with the most powerful family in the High Atlas, the Glaoui, who collaborated with the French and imposed their rule.

Armed by the French and left to their own devices, the Glaoui brothers Madani and T'hami earned a reputation as 'Lords of the High Atlas'. Their tribal base was in Telouet, but they ruled the mountains and the trade routes south of Marrakesh. Even after 1921, when the French sent more soldiers south and extended their influence beyond the mountains, it continued to suit them to exercise power through T'hami el-Glaoui, who then took the title of Pasha of Marrakesh.

Until the period of French control, Marrakesh was mostly confined within its walls, but the colonisers planned European districts – the Ville Nouvelle (New Town) – outside the walls, and the garden suburbs of Guéliz and Hivernage were laid out.

Independence

There was resistance to French rule from the moment it began, but the Moroccan independence movement became viable only after the French defeat by Germany in World War II. However, it wasn't until the early 1950s, when the movement had such popular support that the French felt the need to exile the sultan (later king) Mohammed V to Madagascar, that the outcome became inevitable.

In 1955, Mohammed V returned and in March the following year, choosing to concentrate their efforts on holding Algeria, the French (and soon afterwards the Spanish) recognised Moroccan independence. T'hami el-Glaoui, the Pasha of Marrakesh, who had hoped to exploit the sultan's departure by expanding his influence, died two months before independence but after switching his support to Mohammed V, who was crowned king and oversaw the creation of the modern state.

Hassan II and National Identity

Mohammed V's successor, King Hassan II, who took the throne in 1961, dominated the country for the remainder of the 20th century. Although ostensibly a constitutional monarch,

Hassan II at his first official function, 1961

Hassan ruled the country, forging a renewed national identity for a disparate people that includes Berber tribes in the south, Riffian tribes in the north, the Arab-dominated northern cities and the melting pot of Marrakesh. In 1975, he further enhanced his standing among the people when he used the Spanish withdrawal from the Spanish Sahara as an opportunity to further Morocco's claim to the territory: as the Spanish withdrew, the king encouraged 350,000 Moroccans to occupy the region in what has become known as the *Marche Verte* (Green March). This is an occupation that continues today and is still disputed by several groups, including the United Nations.

A friendly guide sports the fez

Modern Marrakesh

King Hassan II's heir, King Mohammed VI, came to the throne in 1999 and has done much to encourage a more liberal approach to the political system and to search for possible solutions to the continuing Western Sahara dispute. But his most successful policy to date has been his drive to expand tourism in Morocco. Marrakesh has become the epicentre of this development, leading to massive investment, the opening of direct air routes, huge new tourist projects and a welcome rise in employment (as well as a less welcome rise in the cost of living).

Historical Landmarks

1062 The Almoravids, a Berber fundamentalist dynasty founded by Youssef ben Tachfine, establish Marra Kouch (Marrakesh) as their new capital.

1126–7 The first city walls are built.

1147 The Almohads destroy most of the Almoravid monuments, replacing them with their own, including the impressive Koutoubia Mosque.

1184 The city's golden age under Yacoub el-Mansour sees a flourishing of arts and science.

1269 The city goes into decline when the ruling Merenids chose Fez as their capital.

1551 The Saadians re-establish Marrakesh as the capital of an empire that stretches from the Niger river to the Mediterranean.

1578–1603 The great Saadian ruler Ahmed el-Mansour builds the Baadi Palace.

1668 The Alaouite dynasty, from whom the current King Mohammed VI is a descendant, comes to power.

1672 The Alaouite ruler Moulay Ismail moves the capital to Meknes, and the city once again falls into decline for several centuries.

18th–19th centuries Marrakesh is completely dilapidated.

1912 Treaty of Fez makes Morocco a French Protectorate. The French start building a new city (Ville Nouvelle) outside the medina walls.

1918 The French appoint T'hami el-Glaoui as Pasha of Marrakesh and ruler of the south. He and his brother Madani were known as 'Lords of the Atlas' and were notoriously cruel.

1956 Morocco becomes independent under Mohammed V. El-Glaoui dies two months before independence.

1980s Massive rural exodus towards the cities makes Marrakesh Morocco's second largest city.

1999 Mohammed VI becomes king on the death of his father, Hassan II.

2001 First International Film Festival in Marrakesh.

2010 The King hopes to have attracted 10 million visitors a year to Morocco, the culmination of an ambitious tourism development plan.

WHERE TO GO

Most visitors to Marrakesh go in search of the exotic, of sunshine and, increasingly, for the nightlife: but the city also has a good variety of sights that reveal something of its character and bear witness to its rich history. Most of these sights are in the medina (old city), a relatively small area that can be explored easily on foot. This will allow you to take in some shopping in the souks, or enjoy a piping hot mint tea on a café terrace along the way. The souks and the Jemaa el-Fna can become very crowded at times, both with Moroccans and visitors. Fewer people visit the historic monuments and these are often places of peace and tranquillity, where one can recover from the buzz of the city. At first the medina may seem a confusing warren of alleyways and markets, but soon alleys become familiar, other landmarks begin to stand out and the basic ground plan reveals itself, especially as there are only a few main axes through the souks.

The Ville Nouvelle (New Town) has few sights beyond a couple of remarkable gardens. Instead, it is a place to find Western-style shopping and for more varied restaurants and entertainment than are offered in the medina. An afternoon stroll through the streets of the Ville Nouvelle and the neighbouring Hivernage quarter will reveal some well-preserved colonial buildings. The Palmeraie may have lost many of its beautiful palm trees to construction and a withering disease, but it is still a pleasant place for cycling.

For a more thorough glimpse of the countryside around Marrakesh, you need to head a little further afield, to the beautiful fields and gardens of the Ourika Valley or higher up towards the peaks of the Atlas Mountains.

Activity hots up as night falls on 'La Place', Jemaa el-Fna

JEMAA EL-FNA AND AROUND

The medina of Marrakesh is surrounded by well-preserved **city walls** made of *pisé* (clay dried in the sun). These alter their shade with the changing light of the day, from ochre and deep orange to pink and purple. Almoravid Sultan Ali ben Youssef built these 10km (6-mile) long walls in 1126 to protect the city against the threat of the Berbers from Tin-Mal up in the High Atlas. The walls are nearly 10m (33ft) high and have 200 towers and 20 gates. It was once a great outing to cycle or take a horse-drawn carriage (calèche) around the entire medina in the late afternoon light, but the busy road beside it and the heavy traffic now make this less enjoyable. The gates and walls are better explored from inside the medina.

Jemaa el-Fna

The fabulous square of **Jemaa el-Fna** is the heart and soul of the old city and one of the liveliest squares in Morocco, if not in the world. It is the obvious starting point for a tour. The area around it is dotted with budget hotels and small restaurants serving all kinds of delicious food. Overlooking the square is the surviving minaret of the Koutoubia Mosque *(see page 30)*. One of the city's oldest monuments, dating from the 12th century, it is a major landmark that can be seen from almost anywhere in the low-rise city. The elegant tower sits in a beautifully restored garden. Next

Street Food

Boubbouches Snail soup
Brochettes Meat on skewers
Calamars Fried squid
Couscous Steamed semolina with meat and vegetable stew.
Harira Chickpea soup with lamb
Merguez Spicy sausages
Tagine de poulet Chicken stew
Tête d'agneau Sheep's head

Charming a snake in La Place

door, towards the Ville Nouvelle, is the more contemporary Cyber Garden Arsat Moulay Abdel Salam, with efficient public internet booths at its heart. The old and the new cohabit happily in Marrakesh.

The origin of the name of this most famous of Moroccan squares is lost, its meaning disputed. One source translates Jemaa el-Fna as 'Assembly of the Dead', a reference perhaps to the fact that it was used as a place of public executions. But rather than a place of death, 'La Place', as locals refer to it, is very much alive and kicking for most of the day and night: so much so that over the centuries it has become a showcase for popular and traditional culture.

Activity starts early, around 9am, when orange juice vendors set up their stalls. Soon after appear colourful water sellers, who are more likely to make money from the tourists taking pictures than from selling water, along with snake charmers and potion sellers, hoping to attract some

Gnaoua musicians in the square

of the tourists heading across the square to the souks. In the late afternoon the arena in front of the juice stalls becomes busy with storytellers, reciting old Arab tales, with Gnaoua musicians singing their trance songs and acrobats building human pyramids. After the sun goes down the atmosphere becomes even more frenzied with more performers, larger crowds, a cacophony of noises and music, transvestite belly dancers, passionate story tellers and comic acts, all caught up in the swirling smoke and scents of the 100 or so stalls selling excellent street food, from kebabs to a soup of snails.

Recognising its cultural importance, 'La Place' was protected from developers by a preservation order in 1922. In 2001, its importance was further emphasised when Unesco declared it an outstanding example of the world's intangible cultural heritage. It is easy to understand why, for the Jemaa el-Fna is not just part of today's Marrakesh, but captures something of the past and the future, and is a fascinating arena of human interaction.

Try to have at least one meal in the square, sharing a bench with locals around a stallholder grilling meat on skewers or scooping up piles of couscous. Afterwards join the impromptu circles around performers to watch a show. When it all gets too much, head for one of the rooftop terraces around the square for a bird's eye view, and an espresso or a cup of mint tea (no alcohol in these places). Beware of pickpockets at night and the donkey carts and scooters that cross the square, oblivious to the thousands of pedestrians.

Trance Music of the Gnaoua

The musicians on the Jemaa el-Fna, with their castanets, shell-encrusted caps and spinning tassels, may be performing for tourists, but they follow a long tradition. These Gnaoua are descendents of black slaves who were first brought to Morocco in the 16th century when Moroccan control of Timbuktu and the trans-Saharan caravans began. They are mystical healers who, through their music, take possession of the spirits. Using a three-stringed percussive lute (guembri), large metal castanets (qraqeb) and drums (ganga), they create rituals and initiations that are a blend of black African and Arabo-Berber elements. The most important and spectacular ceremony is the Lila Derdeba (The Night of the Stomping of the Feet), an all-night ceremony in which the music and dancing lead to a trance that enables participants to get closer to their mulk, a powerful spirit that possesses them.

Nowadays, they are called upon to perform their trance music for births, weddings and tourist shows. Every year a Gnaoua Festival takes place in Essaouira, where many Gnaoua now work as painters. A group of young musicians, together with Gnaoua masters, have recorded an entire lila (night) of music on the CD Marrakesh Undermoon: the Black Album (www.kamarstudios.com).

Mosque of books

Koutoub is the Arabic for book, and *koutoubiyyin* the word for booksellers. Books, booksellers, printers, binders and scribes occupied the maze of alleys and shops around the original mosque. Appropriately, Sultan Abdel Moumen's offering to celebrate the opening of the new mosque in 1154 was a very early copy of the Koran.

The Koutoubia Mosque

Some 300m/yds southwest of Jemaa el-Fna is the largest tower in Marrakesh, the iconic **minaret** of the **Koutoubia Mosque** (closed to non-Muslims). The elegant minaret, nearly 70m (230ft) high, rises dramatically above the city. A building rule introduced by the French decreed that no building in the medina should be higher than a palm tree, and no building in the Ville Nouvelle higher than the Koutoubia.

The Almohads destroyed the earlier Almoravid mosque and palace, the scattered remains of which can be seen just north of the mosque. The Almohad Sultan Abdel Moumen started building the mosque in 1150 shortly after conquering the city, but he didn't live long enough to complete the minaret; that honour fell to his grandson, Sultan Yacoub el-Mansour (1184–99).

El-Mansour constructed two similar minarets, the Tour Hassan in Rabat and the Giralda in Seville, Spain.

These became the blueprint for minarets in Morocco.

From the **gardens**, you can walk around the outside of the tower. Each facade is decorated with a different pattern, and the ornamentation becomes increasingly rich and fine towards the top, ending in the only surviving strip of the original turquoise faience work. It is believed that the three balls at the pinnacle of the minaret were made of pure gold and were a gift from Yacoub el-Mansour's

Waterseller

wife, who sought forgiveness for breaking the Ramadan fast for three hours. The minaret is floodlit at night and the gardens are open to the public – a great place to hear the *adhan* or call to prayer.

Cyber Garden Arsat Moulay Abdel Salam

The **Cyber Garden Arsat Moulay Abdel Salam,** just north of the Koutoubia Gardens and squeezed between the city walls and Avenue Mohammed V, is another popular public garden. Owned in the 18th century by Moulay Abdel Salam, an Alaouite prince and poet, this beautiful park was brought into the 21st century by the Mohammed VI Foundation for the Protection of the Environment to give the medina more green space. The 8-hectare (20-acre) grounds highlight typical local vegetation: olive groves and orchards intermingle with water features and contemporary areas with grasses and flowers. In an unusual meeting of tradition and innovation, the gardens have at their centre an excellent internet service.

SOUKS

➤ Getting lost in the warren of the **souks** of Marrakesh is one of the city's most memorable experiences. Marrakchis have traded from the city's earliest beginnings: gold, ivory and spices came from Africa, and leather, ceramics and spices went to Europe. It is still the city's mainstay and with so many *riads* in the medina turned into guesthouses or hotels in the last 10 years, there are more customers than ever. As a result, the souks have spread enormously.

The souks are a treat for the senses: the eyes feast on a dazzling display of the best of Morocco's traditional crafts; the

One Aladdin's cave after another

ears ring with noise from the workshops and the constant enticement of vendors trying to sell their wares with 'Entrez, entrez, venez voire pour le plaisir des yeux...' (Come in, come in, for the pleasure of your eyes...); while the nose will take in every smell from the spice market, from the delicate scent of perfume stalls to the pungent odours of the leather tanners. The likelihood is that you will start off energetic and excited, try to keep your spending under control, give in eventually and end up exhausted but happy.

The busiest times in the souks are during the morning and late afternoon, and haggling is very much part of the game when you want to buy something.

There are several entrances to the souk, but the main approach is from the northern side of the Jemaa el-Fna square. It is no longer really necessary to use a guide to the souks. The labyrinthine alleys may be confusing at first but the area is relatively small, and however deep you have ventured you are never much more than a 10-minute walk from 'La Place', which is often signalled by arrows on the wall. If you really get lost, local people are always happy to point you in the right direction. If you have particular items in mind or are planning a big spree, it may be worth spending an afternoon with one of the city's excellent personal shoppers (see page 85).

Souk Smarine and Rakhba Kedima

The easiest way to enter the souk is via an arch on the north side of the Jemaa el-Fna, near the café Terrasses de l'Alhambra *(see page 137)*. The covered market with stalls selling nuts and dried fruits leads to the main artery of the souks, the **Souk Smarine**. This always busy shopping street, broad and well-paved, is mostly devoted to selling souvenirs to tourists, but a few shops still sell wares to local people, including celebratory circumcision outfits for boys. Au Fil d'Or at No. 10 does good-quality traditional clothing for men and women as well as beautiful made-to-measure shirts and jackets.

After about 300m/yds, before the street forks, an alley to the right leads to the lively square of the **Rahba Kedima**. Also known as Place des Epices (Spice Square), this atmospheric open space, once the old corn market, is lined with

Rahba Kedima, or Spice Square

shops selling spices, herbal remedies and a variety of items used in magic potions and amulets, including animal horns, skins, dried lizards, scorpions, hedgehogs and chameleons. Berber women from the Atlas sell their wares, including baskets and hats, from the middle of the square.

On the north side of the square, past the **Café des Epices** *(see panel)*, are two entrance ways to the **Criée Berbère** (Berber Auction). The narrow space is now mostly taken over by carpet sellers, but until 1912 this was the site of a slave auction held every Wednesday, Thursday and Friday before sunset. Slaves captured in Sudan or sub-Saharan Africa were brought to Marrakesh with the camel caravans.

Take a break

Café des Epices *(see page 136)*: sip mint tea while watching the crowds in Rahba Kedima.
Terrace des Epices *(see page 137)*: a peaceful oasis of mint tea, fresh salads and good music in the day, and a cool hangout at night.
Dar Chérifa *(see page 137)*: a lovely literary and arts café.

Kissaria

Just beyond the turn-off to the Rahba Kedima, the Souk Smarine artery divides in two. The alley to the right leads to the **Souk el-Kebir**, the one on the left to the **Souk des Babouches** and further on to the **Souk Kchachbia**. Between the two is the **Kissaria**, a covered market that lies at the heart of the souks. Originally this was a place where the most expensive textiles were sold, but these days it is a place to look for all sorts of fabrics and clothing, and often some less commercial souvenirs.

The Souk el-Kebir still has some woodworkers and wood turners who sell bowls, skewers and other wooden household implements. Further on is the **Souk Cherratine** where there is a traditional saddle maker, and many stalls selling leather goods. At the end of this souk and past the place Ben Youssef, take a right turn on rue Bab Debbagh, and close to the city gate the pungent smell of the nearby **tanneries** will hit you. It's a very smelly but interesting process to watch, even though most natural dyes have these days been replaced by chemicals.

The left-hand alley off that main fork leads into Souk Kchachbia. At first this is called the Souk des Babouches, for obvious reasons: most of the stalls along here are devoted to selling *babouches*, the typical, colourful Moroccan slippers. Further along, a cacophony of beating and hammering will lead you to the dark alley of the **Souk Haddadine** where blacksmiths forge iron into lamp stands, furniture and window grilles that now decorate so many Marrakshi interiors.

Several alleys to the west of Souk Kchachbia lead to the **Souk Sebbaghine** or Dyers' Souk. Wool and scarves in a

Cosmetics in the Spice Market

Arghan oil Locally produced oil of the arghan nut, known for its anti-ageing and anti-oxidising properties.

Cochineal Contained in little pottery saucers and used as lip rouge.

Dadès roses Dried roses and rose water are used to perfume rooms and the body.

Henna Green leaves or powder used to dye the hair, or for tattooing the hands and feet at celebrations.

Kohl Silvery antimony is ground into a powder, which gives a black outline to the eyes and protects them from dust.

Loofah The dried sponge-like fruit of a climbing vine related to the gourd, used as a scrub in bathhouses.

Savon noir Black soap used in the *hammam* (Turkish bath).

Suek Walnut root or bark used as a toothbrush.

rainbow of bright colours are dyed and draped to dry across wires above these picturesque little alleys. There are some junk shops here, and a few shops selling felt bags, carpets and elaborate silverware.

Mouassine

A small alley at the end of the Souk Sebbaghine leads to the crossroads of rue Dar el-Bacha and rue Mouassine. This is the beginning of the up-and-coming **Mouassine** area, with more up-market antique dealers at the far end of rue Dar el-Bacha, as well as several trendy boutiques along the street, on rue Sidi

Coloured wool hung up to dry

el-Yamani and rue el-Ksour. Many caravanserais in the area have been renovated and taken over by shops and workshops. Several European fashion designers have bought properties in this neighbourhood and this is where they shop. As a result of these changes, Mouassine has become the place to look for something unique, although these things tend to come at a price.

The place Bab Ftouh offers another passage between the medina and the Jemaa el-Fna. This little square has many traditional clothing shops as well as a caravanserai where wholesalers sell Berber and other jewellery. Here, too, is the wildly expensive Akbar Delights, which sells exquisite embroidered Indian kaftans and accessories.

THE NORTHERN MEDINA

Just north of the covered souk, the quieter northern part of the medina is more residential, with interesting *riads* turned into bed-and-breakfast accommodation, some down-to-earth food markets and many workshops. The northern medina also includes some important architectural sights. The central square in this quarter is the **place Ben Youssef**.

Medersa Ben Youssef and Koubba Ba'adyin

The green tiled roof and minaret of the **Ben Youssef Mosque**, which is not open for visits, rise above the place Ben Youssef. The Almoravid Sultan Ali Ben Youssef first built a mosque here in the 12th century, but the building standing today dates mostly from the early 19th century.

Across from the mosque is the stunning **Medersa Ben Youssef** (daily Apr–Sept 9am–7pm, Oct–Mar 9am–6pm; charge). *Medersas* (madrassas) were residential colleges for the learning of the Koran, where free board and lodgings were provided to the *tolba* or students. This madrassa was founded in the 14th century by the Merenid Sultan Abou Hassan, and much restored in the 16th century under Saadian Moulay Abdellah, who turned it into the largest example in the country, and one that could rival the Medersa Bou Inania in Fez. As is usual in Islamic architecture, it has plain exterior walls, giving no hint of the staggering ornamentation inside, where every surface is covered in cedar and stucco carvings and *zellige* (mosaic tiling). Intricately executed floral and geometric motifs are repeated in mesmerising patterns, an effect intended to focus the mind on the infinite power and purpose of God. At its height, the monastic-style cells of the Medersa Ben Youssef could house up to 900 students. It remained in use as a religious school until 1962.

From the street, a small passageway leads into a hall from where stairs go up to the *tolba* or students' rooms, arranged around internal lightwells. At the end of the hall is the madrassa's main courtyard, a large open space with a central marble basin, flanked by two galleries of pillars. At the other end is the entrance to the prayer hall, where many classes were held. The prayer hall has an octagonal domed roof supported by marble columns. The arched *mihrab*, which indicates the direction of Mecca, is beautifully decorated with elaborate stucco work.

The madrassa is a marvellous example of Moorish architecture as it developed in Morocco. The building's layout is quite simple, but the proportions are perfect. However, the brilliance of the place lies in its use of decoration. No surface is left untouched and yet the rich and elaborate stucco, cedar carving and *zellij* decoration never overwhelm or

Medersa Ben Youssef

Ben Youssef Mosque

distract from the peace and harmony created by the use of space.

On the south side of the square is the small but historically important **Koubba Ba'adyin** (daily Apr–Sept 9am–7pm, Oct–Mar 9am–6pm; combined charge with Medersa and Musée de Marrakesh), also known as the Almoravid Koubba. The Almoravids introduced many ideas that later became commonplace in Moroccan architecture. The two-storey domed structure covers an ablution pool that appears to be all that has survived of the 12th-century Almoravid Ben Youssef Mosque. It may look insignificant at first sight, but its scalloped and horseshoe arches, stepped, ziggurat-style merlons and fine arabesque patterns are all the more important and poignant in their evocation of the perfection and splendour of that period's Islamic architecture.

Musée de Marrakesh and Dar Bellarj

Past the end of the Souk el-Kebir and just before the Medersa Ben Youssef is the **Musée de Marrakech** (Marrakesh Museum; www.museedemarrakech.ma; daily Apr–Sept 9am–7pm, Oct–Mar 9am–6pm; combined charge, *see above*). The palace of Mehdi M'Nebhi, defence minister and ambassador under Moulay Abdel Aziz, was one of the finest built in Marrakesh in the 19th-century. It was bought by Omar Benjelloun (1928–2003), a passionate collector of traditional Islamic arts, who lovingly restored both the palace and the nearby Medersa Ben Youssef and Koubba Ba'adyin. The museum, opened in 1997, shows temporary exhibitions of traditional and contemporary Moroccan arts.

The M'Nebhi palace is built around a splendid courtyard, with fountains, a pleasant café and a good bookshop. The interior has excellent stucco work and *zellij* tiling and some of the galleries are notable for being in the original *hammam* (bath house) and the *douira* (kitchen).

Behind the Medersa Ben Youssef, **Dar Bellarj** (daily 9am–1.30pm and 2.30–6pm; charge) is a former *fondouk* (caravanserai) that served as a sanctuary for storks *(bellarj)*. The Dar Bellarj Foundation has now restored the property as a cultural centre. The fine building has a peaceful courtyard and is a perfect place to escape the bustle of the souks. It works as an excellent venue for art exhibitions and concerts.

The Seven Men

Marrakesh has had the honour of being the burial place of many holy men. In 1672 Moulay Ismail declared seven of them – Sidi Cadi Ayad, Sidi es-Soheyli, Sidi Yousef bin Ali, Sidi bel Abbès, Sidi bin Sliman el-Jazouli, Sidi Abdal Aziz Tebba and Sidi el-Ghazwani – the patron saints of Marrakesh. They were buried in various cemeteries around the city between the 12th and 16th centuries and a tour of their tombs became a minor pilgrimage, known as the Visit of the Seven Men (es-Sebti) of Marrakesh. This pilgrimage became so famous all over the country that Moroccans sometimes say 'I am going to the Seven Men', meaning that they are travelling to Marrakesh. The pilgrimage ends at the most important shrine, that of Sidi bel Abbès, a 12th-century holy man who was invited to the city by Yacoub el-Mansour.

North of Place Ben Youssef

Rue Bab Taghzout, north of the madrassa and relatively free of tourists, leads to Bab Taghzout and beyond it the **Zaouia of Sidi bel Abbès**, the shrine of the most important of Marrakesh's Seven Saints *(see page 41)*. The large, mainly 18th-century mosque that houses his tomb is off limits to non-Muslims, but it is possible to take a peep at the great pyramid-like shrine. The mosque foundation does a lot of charity work, including the distribution of food to the poor of the neighbourhood.

From there, a street leads eastwards towards **Bab el-Khemis** (Thursday Gate), a fine gate built by the Almohads. Outside it, to the north, is an interesting flea market where many expats and *riad* owners come in search of retro furniture or the odd wall decoration.

West of Place Ben Youssef

Rue Amesfah runs west, behind the Ben Youssef Mosque to the Mouassine quarter. Past rue Riad el-Arous lies the **Zaouia of Sidi Abdel Aziz**, the shrine of another of the Seven Saints, who died in 1508. Nearby is the ornate **Mouassine Fountain** and further left the **Mouassine Mosque** (closed to non-Muslims), built by Saadian Sultan Abdullah el-Ghalib in 1560. Further east lies the **Dar el-Bacha** (also known as Dar el-Glaoui; daily 9am–noon and 3–6pm; charge). This was the palace of the despotic and cruel T'hami el-Glaoui *(see page 20)* who ruled Marrakesh and the Atlas for the French under the Protectorate. When he died in 1956 the building was plundered with a vengeance. One of the city's most opulent buildings, it was restored and set up as a museum in 2007 by the late Patty Cadby Birch, an American collector of Islamic fine art and antiquities, whose beautiful *riad*, Dar Kandi, was built in 1915 for one of the Glaoui brothers.

THE SOUTHERN MEDINA

The Almohads under Sultan Yacoub el-Mansour first built their **Kasbah**, or walled citadel, in the southern part of the medina during the 12th century. The complex included palaces, barracks and the royal mosque. Successive rulers all made their mark by building over and adding to the splendour of the imperial city. The Kasbah still holds the royal palace used today by King Mohammed VI when he is in town (closed to visitors). This is also where Sultan Ahmed el-Mansour built the el-Badi Palace, appropriately called 'the Incomparable'. The Saadians also chose to bury their sultans here, in the magnificent Saadian Tombs *(see page 45)*.

Next to the Kasbah is the old Jewish quarter, the **Mellah**, with narrow alleys, old synagogues and a spice market.

Bab Agnaou, entrance to the Kasbah

Mosquée de la Kasbah

At the heart of the southern medina, the lively place des Ferblantiers has been spruced up in recent years. From there the parallel streets rue Riad Zitoun el-Kedim and rue Riad Zitoun el-Jdid lead straight to the Jemaa el-Fna. The quarter is most easily visited on foot.

Bab Agnaou

The main gate into the medina was the **Bab er-Rob**, but nearby **Bab Agnaou** gave entrance to the Kasbah. This elegant gate was ordered by the Almohad Sultan Yacoub el-Mansour in 1185 and, exceptionally for Marrakesh, was not built in pink *pisé* but carved in the local blue-greyish Guéliz stone, from a quarry north of Marrakesh. Agnaou in Berber means 'a ram without horns', referring to the fact that the gate lost its two towers, but it is more commonly believed that it means 'Gate of the Guineans', a reference to the royal guards who were brought from sub-Saharan Africa.

Immediately inside the gate is the **Mosquée de la Kasbah** (no entry for non-Muslims), which was also built by Sultan Yacoub el-Mansour and is easily recognisable by the original green tiles that decorate the minaret. This vast mosque, which has five inner courtyards, was restored by the Saadians and, more recently, by the late King Hassan II, which is why it looks so new. The domed *mihrab*, the niche indicating the direction of Mecca, is supported by four columns.

Saadian Tombs

Part of the mosque complex is an enclosed garden, now planted with trees and rosemary. The descendants of Prophet Mohammed, known as *shorfa*, had long been buried in this garden, often in anonymous tombs, and the 16th-century Saadians chose the same place to bury their own sultans and their families. The dynasty's founder, Sultan Mohammed esh-Sheikh, was buried here in 1557, in a simple domed tomb. Most of the exquisitely decorated *koubbas*, standing today, were built by his third son, the great conqueror Ahmed el-Mansour, for himself and his immediate family. As the garden cemetery was only accessible through the mosque, the dead sultans rested in peace. Unlike the Badi Palace, which was dismantled by the later Sultan Moulay Ismail and his Alaouite successors, the Saadian Tombs escaped pilfering. They disappeared in the overgrown garden and were almost forgotten until the French General

The Saadian Tombs and garden

Lyautey had the area surveyed from the air in 1917, and then cut a new narrow entrance through the wall. The restored **Saadian Tombs** (daily 8.30–11.45am and 2.30–5.45pm; charge) are now one of the major attractions in town, so go early in the morning or late afternoon to avoid the coach parties.

The first hall to the left is the **prayer hall**. Four pillars support lofty horseshoe arches and there's a finely decorated *mihrab*. Ahmed el-Mansour connected this hall to his own tomb but didn't intend it as a burial place. Later rulers, however, were buried here, including several 18th-century Alaouite princes.

Hall of Twelve Columns, Saadian Tombs

An elegant arch opposite the *mihrab* leads to the central mausoleum of Ahmed el-Mansour, known as the **Hall of Twelve Columns**. The central tombs, flanked by 12 decorated marble columns, hold the remains of Ahmed el-Mansour, who died in 1603, with his son Zaidan to his right and grandson Mohammed esh-Sheikh II to the left. The decoration of the gilded cedar wood dome is overwhelmingly rich, with some stunning calligraphy, while the walls are covered in splendid *zellij* mosaic. Thirty-three other princes are buried here, and more in the **Hall of the Three Niches** to the right.

The **Second Koubba** in the middle of the garden was the first one to be built by the Ahmed el-Mansour, and is more sober in decoration. The burial chamber, decorated with *muqarnas* (stalactites), contains the tomb of his mother, the venerated Lalla Messaouda, with a commemorative inscription. To her left is the tomb of his half-brother Sultan Abdullah el-Ghalib, and to his left the tomb of his father Mohammed esh-Sheikh. Only the torso of his father is buried here, as the Turkish mercenaries who killed him took his head to be displayed in Istanbul.

The Mellah and Place des Ferblantiers

From the garden entrance, return to Bab Agnaou, turn right onto rue Oqba ben Nafaa and right again on avenue Houmman el-Fetouaki, which leads to the **place des Ferblantiers** (Tinsmiths' Square) and the **Mellah**.

The picturesque square, once part of a souk in the Jewish quarter or *mellah*, is a large *fondouk* (caravanserai) now taken over by lantern makers. The square has been restored and cleaned up in recent years, and is now a pleasant place for a drink and snack on one of the café terraces. You could also head for the rooftop of the trendy Kosybar *(see page 138)*. Across the street is a covered market with gold jewellery shops and a few silver dealers.

Star of David tiles in Mellah

To the east, through the **Bab Berrima** gate, lies the Mellah. In 1558, nearly 100 years later than most other Moroccan cities, the Saadian Sultan Abdullah el-Ghalib moved all the Jews of Marrakesh into the Mellah, a secure quarter adjacent to the royal palace, entered by just two gates. The Mellah

The royal palace of el-Badi

formed a city within the city, governed by a council of rabbis, which was led by a Jewish *Qaid* (leader). The Mellah had its own souk, gardens and cemetery. The Jews were very influential traders and bankers under the Saadians and often made a living as middlemen between Muslim and Christian merchants. Before World War II, more than 16,000 Jews lived in the high buildings in this quarter, but after 1948 and the foundation of Israel many of them moved either there or to more cosmopolitan Casablanca. Today, fewer than 200 Jews remain in Marrakesh, and the Mellah is now mostly inhabited by Muslims. Several synagogues can still be visited, including **Bitton** (rue Touareg), **Bethel** and **Lazama** (36 Derb Ragraga; Sun–Thur 9am–6pm, Fri 9am–1pm; tip expected). Several guides will offer to show you around for a tip or you can find information at the **Community Office** (142 avenue Houmane el-Fetouaki). To the east is the well-kept Jewish cemetery of Miâara (Sun–Thur 7am–6pm, Fri

7am–3pm; tip expected), believed to date from the 17th century, and including the 11 shrines of Jewish *marabouts* (holy men).

El-Badi Palace

The Bab Berrima leads to a double-walled street, which in turn leads straight ahead to the **El-Badi Palace** (daily 8.30–11.45am and 2.30–5.45pm; charge), recognisable from the many storks' nests that top the wall.

Ahmed el-Mansour came to the throne in 1578 after the Battle of the Three Kings – King Sebastian of Portugal and his Moroccan ally Abu Abdallah Mohammed II Saadi, who wanted to recover his throne from his uncle Abd Al-Malik Saadi. All three died in battle but the Portuguese were defeated and the Moroccans acquired great wealth from ransoms and captured treasures. Just five months after the battle, Ahmed el-Mansour, 'the Victorious', started building this palace, which deserved its name 'the Incomparable', a very worldly use of one of the 99 names of Allah. In 1598 Ahmed el-Mansour captured Timbuktu and acquired so much wealth that he was given yet another title, ed-Dahabi or 'the Golden'.

The king employed the best craftsmen and bought the finest materials. It is said that he exchanged Italian marble for Moroccan sugar from the Souss Valley, pound for pound, and that his quest for precious materials went as far as China. Walls and ceilings were covered with gold from Timbuktu, sunken gardens were filled with perfumed flowers, the central pool was 90m (300ft) long with an island in the middle: everything was as lavish as it could be. The palace took 25 years to build, and although it was finished only a few months before al-Mansour's death in 1603, he threw plenty of extravagant parties and celebrations for the inauguration. Allegedly, when the old sultan asked his joker what he thought of the palace, the fool answered that it would

Sacred storks

In Moroccan culture, storks, which are often seen nesting on rooftops, minarets and walls, are considered a sign of good fortune. Berbers believe that storks are transformed humans. In *The Garden of Secrets* the Spanish writer Juan Goytisolo alludes to this belief, and tells the story of the Stork-Man.

make a big pile of stones if it were demolished. Little did he know that 90 years later Moulay Ismail would destroy the palace, and that it would take him 12 years to strip all its precious materials. He built himself a fine palace in Meknes with the 'big pile of stones'.

Moulay Ismail did a definitive job, and visitors must use their imagination to envisage the splendour of what was one of the most magnificent palaces ever constructed. The original entrance was from the gatehouse in the southeast corner, but today the entrance is on the north side.

The palace's **central courtyard** is massive, with five basins and four sunken gardens planted with orange trees. They would have been typical Moorish gardens with cypresses, palms, olive trees and perfumed flowers as well as citrus trees. On each side of the courtyard was a pavilion. The largest on the western side was the **Koubba el-Hamsiniya** (Pavilion of 50 Columns) and opposite it the Crystal Pavilion. To the north was the **Green Pavilion**, and south the **Koubba Khaysuran**, named after the sultan's favourite wife and now an exhibition space for local artists. In the northeastern corner a staircase gives access to the rooftop terrace with great views over the vastness of the complex and the rest of the medina.

The Minbar

The 12th-century minbar (stepped pulpit) of the Koutoubia Mosque, a marvel of medieval Islamic art, is on display in an annex in the southeastern corner. It was built in Córdoba for an Almoravid mosque, but after destroying that building the conquering Almohad rulers moved it into an enclosure in their new mosque. After this mosque was found to be incorrectly directed towards Mecca and destroyed, the minbar was moved to the Koutoubia Mosque. In 1996 a US-led team worked on the conservation of the masterpiece, moving it to the Baadi palace. Originally every bit of surface was covered with carved wooden panels and intricate marquetry, of which some of the 1.3 million pieces were tinier than a grain of rice. All were clearly carved by the greatest masters of the time.

Today the Baadi palace is used as a venue for an annual music festival and during the International Film Festival (*see page 94*). The ruins get pretty hot during the day so be sure to bring drinking water and sun protection.

The stork is said to bring good luck

El-Bahia Palace

El-Bahia Palace

North of the place des Ferblantiers are two parallel streets that both run to the Jemaa el-Fna. These are the **rue Riad Zitoun el-Kedim** (Street of the Old Olive Grove) and **rue Riad Zitoun el-Jdid** (Street of the New Olive Grove). The first street starts off with shops selling interesting picture frames and small pieces of furniture made from recycled car tyres, and becomes a budget hotel haven when it gets closer to Jemaa el-Fna.

At the top of rue Riad Zitoun el-Jdid, on the corner, is another palace, **El-Bahia** or 'the Brilliant' (Sat–Thur 8.45–11.45am and 2.45–5.45pm, Fri 8.45–11.30am and 3–5.45pm; charge). El-Bahia was built by two generations of 19th-century grand viziers, a ranking similar to prime minister. Si Moussa, who started building in the 1860s, was grand vizier to Sultan Sidi Mohammed ben Abdehrahmane, and his son Ba Ahmed served Sultan Moulay Hassan, and was regent for the child sultan Abdul Aziz.

Sultan Abdul Aziz is said to have become so jealous of his vizier's fortunes that when Ba Ahmed died, he forced the family, who included four wives and 24 concubines, to leave. When the staff started stripping the palace, the sultan stopped them, only to collect all the booty for himself. The Bahia palace extended over 8 hectares (20 acres), and its complicated plan included a series of courtyards, gardens, pavilions and 150 rooms. One can almost smell the intrigue that must have been rife here.

The infamous warlord Madani Glaoui lived here from 1908 until 1911, when it became the residence of the French Résident-Général under the Protectorate.

Only part of the empty palace can be visited, as some of it is still used by the current royal family and their staff. King Mohammed VI threw a lavish party here for the rapper P. Diddy a few years ago. The entrance is from the western side and although the layout is rather confusing, the gardens and courtyards are tranquil and utterly delightful.

Museum Street

Further north along rue Riad Zitoun el-Jdid, opposite the small parking area, are signs for two interesting museums, housed in grand *riads*. The **Dar Si Said Museum** (rue Kennaria; daily 9am–noon and 3–6pm; charge) is in a modest palace built by Si Said, the mentally defective brother of Ba Ahmed, who built the Bahia Palace next door. The building is small and far more intimate than the vast neighbouring palace, and it has some gorgeous, ornate painted ceilings and fine woodwork. The museum houses an important collection of decorative arts and crafts from the south of the country. The room closest to the entrance is lined with some beautiful wooden doors rescued from kasbahs and old medina houses.

Archway in Dar Si Said Museum

Further along is the oldest item in the museum's collection: a fine 10th-century marble fountain basin brought to Marrakesh from Córdoba. Near the pleasant courtyard stands an ancient-looking ferris wheel that was used to entertain children during *moussems* or saints' festivals until the 1970s. Around the courtyard are rooms holding rich displays of southern Moroccan jewellery, with filigree silver from the Jbel Siroua, fibules from Tiznit and ornate powder horns and daggers. Also interesting is the carpet collection, which clearly demonstrates the style differences between Berber and Arab carpets. The Berber carpets, or *hanbels*, are more colourful and employ mainly geometric patterns; while those made by the Arab tribes, in dark reds and purples, have more chaotic designs and are traditionally narrower as they were made to fit their tents. The last room contains some exquisite carved cedar woodwork, some rescued from the el-Badi palace.

Nearby is **Maison Tiskiwine** (8 derb el-Bahia; daily 9.30am–12.30pm and 3.30–6pm; charge), the private house and collection of long-time Marrakesh resident, the Dutch anthropologist Bert Flint. He has collected tribal art for decades and has organised the exhibition geographically as a journey along the old trade routes between Marrakesh and Timbuktu. He is passionate about his mission to point out that Marrakesh is more African than Arabic in its roots, and he illustrates here the city's strong historic link with Timbuktu. The museum receives relatively few visitors, but is very compelling, with displays of colourful and fine pottery, jewellery, textiles and carpets. Getting off the busy streets one enters another space and time. One starts envisaging what it was like to be a trader, travelling in one of the camel caravans, and encountering many different tribes on the way. The journey ends in Timbuktu, represented by Flint's peaceful courtyard filled with bird song.

Place de la Liberté

GUÉLIZ AND HIVERNAGE

When the French arrived early in the 20th century and made Morocco their Protectorate, they turned up their noses at the native quarters within the walls and decided to build their new town, as elsewhere in Morocco, outside the walls. This *ville nouvelle* was elegant, with wide avenues, large villas surrounded by gardens and serene parks. Later on, wealthy Moroccans moved out of the medina as well, into flats and houses in the new town to which they could easily drive. In the 1970s most visitors stayed in Guéliz as the medina was too much of a hassle, but that changed in the 1990s when people started renovating *riads*. The trend is turning again, as in recent years the medina is becoming more crowded, the enclosed *riads* too claustrophobic, and the art deco and modernist architecture of Guéliz is again becoming the flavour of the moment.

Take a calèche – a good way to get about town

The new town divides into Guéliz, the lively area centred on avenue Mohammed V, and the quieter Hivernage which has plenty of large villas and many hotels. The *ville nouvelle* has a wealth of colonial architecture and offers visitors a chance to escape the narrow alleys and souks for Western-style shopping, fine dining and increasingly good nightlife.

► Guéliz

The 3km (2-mile) long broad avenue that runs right through Marrakesh, from the Koutoubia Mosque to the Jbel Guéliz (Mount Guéliz), is the buzzing **avenue Mohammed V**. About 400m/yds west of the Koutoubia Mosque is the **Ensemble Artisanal**, where craftsmen, including lantern makers, leather workers, woodworkers, weavers and jewellers, have workshops and sell their goods, perhaps at a slightly higher but fixed price. So it's a good place to get an idea of price and quality before you start bargaining in the souks.

On the opposite side of the road is the **Cyber Garden Arsat Moulay Abdel Salam** *(see page 31)*. There are three major roundabouts along avenue Mohammed V: the **place de la Liberté** with a large fountain, the **place du 16 Novembre**, the heart of Guéliz, with the main post office, and the **place Abdelmoumen Ben Ali** lined by café terraces, the most popular of which is the **Café des Négociants**.

Just west of the place de la Liberté is the **Eglise des Saints-Martyrs de Marrakech** (rue el-Imam, Guéliz; services Mon–Sat 6.30pm, Sun 10am), the *église* (church) from which Guéliz took its name. It was built in 1930 by the French, and dedicated to five 13th-century Franciscan friars who were beheaded in Muslim Seville for preaching Christianity. The stark, impressive facade translates into a cool spacious interior, decorated only by the sunlight streaming through the coloured stained glass. Nearby, off the place du 16 Novembre, is the **Jnane el-Harti**, a small park originally laid out by the French as a formal garden and zoo. Re-landscaped and with a children's play area and fountains, this is a popular place for an early evening stroll.

Further west is the splendid **Théâtre Royal** (avenue de France; daily 8.30am–7pm; free) inaugurated in 2001. Designed by one of Morocco's leading architects, Charles Boccara, it has a classical portico and dome, and an auditorium linked by a courtyard to the 1,200-seat open-air theatre. The theatre is only sporadically used, but exhibitions by local and visiting artists fill the exhibition hall.

Street sign on the busy avenue

Most of the up-market shopping and trendy restaurants are around the **place Abdelmoumen Ben Ali** and what was the old **Marché Central** (Central Market) which was destroyed a few years ago, and moved into a lesser building on rue Ibn Toumert, behind the huge Marrakesh Plaza on place du 16 Novembre – a good place to stock up for a picnic. This stretch of avenue Mohammed V, as well as the area around the **rue de Yougoslavie** and **rue de la Liberté**, has numerous examples of colonial 'Mauresque' architecture, a blend of French-European architecture with Moorish influences. The small **Spanish Quarter** just west of the rue de Yougoslavie, with diverse, colourful single-storey cottages, is all that is left of the large Spanish population that once lived here.

North of boulevard Mohammed Zerktouni is another reminder of colonial days, the large **European Cemetery** (rue Er-Rouada; Apr–Sept 7am–7pm, Oct–Mar 8am–6pm; free), which dates from the 1920s. The overgrown cemetery, a

The New Royal Road

Just as his grandfather gave his name to the city's commercial artery, the avenue Mohammed V, so the young King Mohammed VI has given his to the old avenue de France. So far its claim to fame is that it is 'the longest avenue in Africa', and the 8km (5-mile) street will be a showcase for the king's vision of the future of Marrakesh. It starts in the north at the intersection of the route de Targa and runs through new residential areas until it crosses avenue Hassan II, where the old colonial railway station is undergoing a grand restoration and the great theatre built by Charles Boccara (see page 57) stands empty. The street continues past the vast new conference centre, the Palais des Congrès, past luxury hotels and what is to be the new Zone Touristique, with endless tourist developments that will help fulfill the king's dream of luring 10 million tourists to Morocco by 2010.

Chic French-style shopping

romantic and peaceful place that is rarely visited, contains the tombs of the *colons* and has a white obelisk reminding visitors of the North African soldiers who died fighting in World War II to free France. A few minutes' walk eastwards is the delightful **Majorelle Garden** *(see page 63)*.

Hivernage

South of Guéliz, **Hivernage** was built as an intimate garden suburb, with large villas surrounded by greenery. Stroll around the narrow winding streets and have a drink in the area's oldest hotel, the **Saadi**, set in mature gardens, which recently opened a luxurious new annex somehow resembling a pre-war Baghdad more than Marrakesh. Several long-established restaurants include **Le Comptoir** *(see page 141)*, the nightspot with the hottest belly dancers in town. Further west lie the large, pleasant **Menara Gardens** *(see page 62)*.

Agdal Gardens with the Atlas Mountains in the distance

GARDENS

Gardens are hugely important in Islamic culture, as they are thought to be the realisation on Earth of paradise as it is described in the Koran. Large royal gardens and small internal courtyard gardens alike are places full of shade, birdsong, perfume, beauty and pleasure, but they are also considered to be places where heaven meets earth, infinity meets the temporary and God and mankind come into contact.

In the past Marrakesh has often been described as a huge palm grove; as a garden with surprisingly lush vegetation in a region with so little water. The secret behind the gardens and the Palmeraie (palm grove) was the water brought from the Atlas Mountains, or from underground water sources by *khettaras* (underground water channels) – a system the Moroccans borrowed from the ancient Persians, via the Arabs. The Palmeraie and other gardens have suffered considerably in recent decades, mainly because of the rapid expansion of the city, but the gardens still open to visitors offer a welcome respite from the heat and the buzz of the city, and still convey a sense of beauty and tranquillity.

The Palmeraie

Marrakesh's **Palmeraie** once spread over more than 13,000 hectares (32,000 acres), and it was estimated that it had about 150,000 palm trees, all watered by the *khettaras*. Legend has it that it was created by the date pips casually thrown aside by the Arab soldiers camping outside the city before conquering it, but it seems probable that a lot more effort than that was required.

The Palmeraie has undergone a lot of change in recent years. The *khettara* system no longer functions and water is provided by artesian wells; the date palms all over North Africa have suffered from a virus; and, most significantly, large plots of land were sold off to build luxury hotels and large villas for Moroccan and foreign celebrities. It used to be pleasant to cycle through the winding lanes in the shade of palms, but it is less exotic now. It is fine as a place for a late afternoon stroll, but the main attraction these days is to sit by a pool on a hot day. The luxury **Jnane Tamsna** guesthouse is set in a lovely garden filled with fruit trees, rosemary bushes and organic vegetables, lovingly designed by the owner, ethno-botanist Gary Martin. It offers a set menu lunch made from garden produce, as well as a day at the pool (*see page 134*). The über-trendy **Nikki Beach** *(see page 90)* is another pleasant oasis. The Palmeraie is not called the 'Beverly Hills of Morocco' for nothing.

Agdal

Just south of the medina, the **Agdal Garden** (Fri and Sun, closed if the king is in residence; free) was originally spread over 500 hectares (1,200 acres), more or less the same area as the entire medina. It was laid out by the Almohad rulers, at the back of the royal palace, in 1156. At the centre is a huge pool, the **Sahraj el-Hana** (The Tank of Health), in which the 19th-century Sultan Mohammed IV tragically drowned while rowing with his son. Around the pool are different kinds of orchards, including a palm grove, oranges, figs, pomegranates, vines and walnut trees, as well as several ornamental pavilions. You can climb onto the roof of the one beside the pool for a great view over the garden, against the dramatic backdrop of the High Atlas Mountains.

Menara

The **Menara** (avenue de la Ménara, Hivernage; daily 5am–6.30pm; free but charge for picnic pavilion) very much follows the plan of the quintessential Islamic garden, with

Reflections in the Menara

orchards, pools and a pavilion. It is a vast garden with
age-old olive trees. The gardens were also designed by
the Almohads during the
12th century, and have a
central basin, 200m (650ft)
long and 150m (500ft) wide,
fed by underground chan-
nels. It is a popular picnic
spot for Marrakchis, and at
night the pool is lit for the
Marvels and Reflection

Majorelle Garden

show (Apr–May and Aug daily 10pm; Mar, June–July and
Sept–Dec Mon–Sat 10pm; charge), which features music,
dancers and acrobats.

Majorelle Garden

The jewel in the crown of Marrakesh gardens, is the well-
kept **Majorelle Garden** (avenue Yaqoub el-Mansour; www.
jardinmajorelle.com; daily June–Sept 8am–6pm, Oct–May
8am–5pm; charge, additional charge for Islamic Museum).
It was created in the 1930s by the French artist Jacques Majorelle and his son Louis, and later purchased by French fashion designer Yves Saint Laurent (who died in June 2008) and
his partner Pierre Bergé, who had a villa next door.

Jacques Majorelle came to Marrakesh in 1919 to recover from heart problems, and fell in love with the light and
the colours. He bought the land in 1924 and designed an
exotic botanical garden around his studio. The cactus garden has species from all over the world and looks monu-
mental against the electric blue *(see page 64)*. Other
features are the spectacular bougainvillea and a rustling
bamboo forest, interspersed with pools filled with water

Majorelle blue

Jacques Majorelle gave his name to the electric cobalt blue with which he painted the exterior of his studio, setting off the green of the garden perfectly. Some say it was inspired by the blue of French workmen's overalls, others claim he was inspired by Berber homes in the south.

lilies and lively with frogs. His studio now houses a small **Islamic Museum**, with some of his own work, and a beautiful collection of Berber jewellery, magnificent carved doors and fine textiles. The small **boutique** sells books, jewellery and good-quality crafts. The gardens are increasingly popular so visit early in the morning or late afternoon. The small café in the garden serves a good breakfast until 11.30am as well as salads and snacks for lunch.

Mamounia

The grand old dame of Marrakesh, the **Hotel Mamounia** (avenue Bab Jdid, southern medina; www.mamounia.com) has been under restoration for a while, and in true Marrakchi style, rumours are rife about its transformation and predicted opening. It certainly looks as if it might take a while. The mature garden is said to have inspired Winston Churchill to start painting watercolours, and he described it to his friend Franklin D. Roosevelt as 'the loveliest spot in the world'. The name comes from Arset el-Mamoun, as the gardens were called in the 18th century by the Saadian Crown Prince Moulay Mamoun, who received the land as a wedding gift from his father. The hotel was built in the early 20th century when Morocco came under French rule. The gardens kept their traditional design with walkways, orange and olive groves, rose beds, and some of the most majestic palm trees in town. When the hotel re-opens it will be possible to have a drink or meal in the garden.

Beldi Country Club

The newest garden in town is the vast expanse of the **Beldi Country Club** (route du Barrage, Cherifia; www.beldicountry club.com; charge includes set menu lunch, additional charge for use of the swimming pool), set in more than 7 hectares (17 acres) of land. Some 6km (4 miles) south of Marrakesh, it was opened in 2006 by a Moroccan-born Frenchman and a Moroccan gardener. The gardens are stunning, with a *roseraie* of 12,000 rose bushes, as well as ancient olive trees, cacti and a vegetable garden.

'Beldi' means 'from the countryside' and everything is done to keep the gardens, restaurant and small guesthouse (due to open December 2008) as rural and simple as possible. A spa *(see page 89)* using aromatic oils and herbs has just opened and there are plans for an additional botanical garden spread over 8 hectares (20 acres).

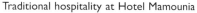

Traditional hospitality at Hotel Mamounia

EXCURSIONS FROM MARRAKESH

One of the great sights in Marrakesh, but due to the haze of pollution one that is now not so often seen, is the backdrop of the snowy peaks of the nearby High Atlas. The city may be expanding fast, and becoming busier and more noisy every day, but one of its attractions is that it still needs only a quick ride out of town to be in the empty countryside or way up in the mountains.

The most obvious escape is towards the Ourika Valley for a picnic or a walk, or a swim in the **Lalla Takerkoust Lake**, and in winter there is the option of skiing in **Oukaimeden**. The **High Atlas** offers endless opportunities for hiking, horse riding or visiting weekly rural souks, and to the east of Marrakesh are the famous **Ouzoud Waterfalls**. For a breath of fresh sea air, the obvious choice is the old fishing port of **Essaouira**.

Many visitors book a room in a *riad* for a week, and start feeling claustrophobic after three days. In recent years many hotels and bed-and-breakfasts have opened outside Marrakesh, many operators offer sports activities in the countryside around the city *(see pages 90–2)*, country clubs and private beaches attract sun seekers and the mountains offer numerous possibilities to escape the city.

Ourika Valley

Lake Lalla Takerkoust and Ourika Valley

The artificial **Lake Lalla Takerkoust**, formed by the dam built by the French between 1929 and 1935 to provide Marrakesh with electricity, is only 40km (25 miles) away. The lake has become increasingly popular over the past few years and has seen the opening of several restaurants and guesthouses around it, as well as private and public beaches on its shores. This is a popular summer excursion and there are several refreshing options for cooling down in the water, as well as swimming: pedal boats, kayaks, windsurf boards and even jet skis. Those looking for peace and quiet are better off heading for the northern side of the lake.

South of Marrakesh and about 20km (12 miles) east of the lake is the beautiful and easy-to-access **Ourika Valley**. Many Marrakchis have a second home or farm in this valley, and more and more expats are selling up in the medina for the peace and quiet here. The temperature in summer is far more agreeable, often 10 to 15°C (50–59°F) cooler, and the river banks are a popular spot in summer for picnicking or camping. It is a good place to go for the day, or spend a few days trekking.

The Ourika Road (P2017) leads south of Marrakesh to the Ourika Valley, and after 34km (21 miles) is the village of **Tnine-l'Ourika**. The village has a great souk on Monday, but you need to get there early before the crowds arrive. Signposted from the village is the **Jardin du Safran** (www.safran-ourika.com; daily 8.30am–6pm; charge), which offers guided tours of the farm where the purple flowers of the *Crocus*

The Monday market, Trine-l'Ourika

sativus, which originally came from Kashmir and Nepal, produce excellent saffron. The plants only flower for 20 days a year, usually the three first weeks of November, and 140 flowers are needed for 1g of saffron.

Nearby, in the same village, is another perfumed garden, the **Jardins Bio-aromatiques de l'Ourika** (www.nectarome.com; daily Mar–July and Sept 9am–

Setti Fatma's saint

Every year in mid-August the village of Setti Fatma celebrates the *moussem* (saint's day) of the local saint after whom the village is named. It's a joyful occasion and families from the whole area attend, both for the religious Sufi gatherings and to visit the huge souk where a variety of performers entertain the crowds.

7pm, Oct–Feb 9am–5pm; charge) where 50 different plants are grown for the production of organic essential oils and bath products, which are for sale in the shop. You can visit these wonderful gardens alone or with a guided tour (1–1½ hours). The best time to visit is in spring, between March and June.

From here the Ourika river winds through orchards, gardens and fields, with great views of picturesque *douars*, tiny *pisé* villages. At the lovely village of **Aghbalou**, the road divides in two with the left turn going to **Setti Fatma** and the right to the ski and trekking resort of **Oukaimeden**. Setti Fatma is a pretty village with many opportunities for trekking. The most popular option is the walk to the **Seven Falls**, about four hours away, for a swim and a picnic, but for longer treks contact the **Bureau des Guides** in the village. Oukaïmeden, 75km (46 miles) south of Marrakesh, is Africa's highest ski station at 2,600m (8,500ft), with pistes of all levels. There is snow from mid-December until mid-April, but for the rest of the year it is a good base for walking *(see page 91)*.

Snowy peaks of Mount Toubkal

High Atlas

The wildest place to escape to from Marrakesh is undoubtedly the **Toubkal National Park** in the **High Atlas**. The road up to Asni is at first uneventful but soon becomes dramatic, with superb views of the fertile river valley and mud-brick villages clinging to the hillside. **Asni** is the first main village along the road, 47km (29 miles) south of Marrakesh. It is a Berber village, famous for its large **Saturday souk**, which attracts tour groups from Marrakesh. Bargain hard for what you want, it's part of the game, and watch out for so-called Berbers approaching with old silver jewellery, who then propose lunch at their family home or a walk – many people have been tricked out of money in this way. A spectacular road leads through deep gorges and lush mountain scenery to Imlil, 17km (10 miles) away. **Imlil** is the main starting point for climbing North Africa's highest peak, Jbel Toubkal (4,167m/13,666ft), a popular three- to four-day climb. The village is well set up with a **Bureau des Guides** and shops to stock up on food. A good walk for the day is to **Aremd** (one hour from Imlil) and another 1½ hours to **Sidi Chamarouch** at 2,600m (8,500ft), the shrine of the saint of the same name, who is believed to cure psychiatric problems.

Many visitors from Marrakesh head for the pleasant surroundings of the **Kasbah du Toubkal** (www.kasbahdu toubkal.com), just above the village of Imlil. This wonderful eco-lodge is the brainchild of Mike McHugo together with the local berbers. The former summer lodge of the local ruler has spectacular views over the surrounding mountains, and is a place of serenity and retreat. Lunch, served on the rooftop terrace in good weather, is a simple Berber-style meal served by friendly villagers. The lodge has luxurious rooms as well as dormitories for students, but many people just go for lunch and a brisk walk.

Back towards Asni, and continuing further south along the main road, is the village of **Ouirgane** (60km/37 miles from Marrakesh), in the middle of an alpine landscape. So far this is a quiet village and a good base for treks in the gorgeous surroundings, but a new dam has created a lake, and that brings with it the promise of huge tourist developments and noisier times ahead. The N10, which continues towards the **Tizi-n-Test**, is one of the most beautiful roads in Morocco.

After Ouirgane the road enters the **N'Fis Gorges**, and then follows the **Agoundis River** valley, dotted by **kas-**

Kasbah du Toubkal

bahs that belonged to the powerful Goundafa Berber tribe who controlled this region in the 19th century.

Forty kilometres (25 miles) after Ouirgane, commanding the area high up on the opposite river bank is the splendid **mosque of Tin-Mal** (daily; charge). The 12th-century mosque is all that remains of the Almohad city of Tin-Mal, and it is one of only two mosques non-Muslims can enter in Morocco. Built in 1156 in honour of the Almohads spiritual leader, Mohammed ibn Tumert, the mosque, which resembles a kasbah, has an interior of austere beauty, with a pleasing purity of line. Climb to the top of the minaret for wonderful views over the valley and mosque.

Cascades d'Ouzoud

The road was recently repaired and the mosque has been restored but it still sees relatively few visitors, so if the door is closed call the guard (tel: 062-725612).

Cascades d'Ouzoud

The **Cascades d'Ouzoud** (Ouzoud Falls), 165km (100 miles) northeast of Marrakesh, are a popular day trip for Marrakchis, who come for a family lunch and to enjoy the cooling waters of Morocco's biggest waterfall. The water of the Oued Ouzoud (River of Olives) plunges down 110m (360ft) in three main tiers, past lush vegetation, and then into an idyllic pool overlooked by several café terraces serving good *tagines* and drinks. The afternoon sun glinting in the spray makes for a magic rainbow, and the roar of the falling water is soothing for the soul. The falls are most spectacular between March and June. The place gets busy at weekends and in summer when Moroccan students camp nearby, but

for most of the year it is easy to feel the appeal of this place, which is like a perfect image of paradise hidden deep in the Atlas mountains. Views of the falls from above are beautiful, but walk down to the bottom for the full effect. The currents make it dangerous to swim in the plunge pool, but it is delightful to do so in the icy-cold pools downstream.

Those with itchy feet can go for a walk, following the river downstream about 3km (2 miles) to the photogenic old Berber village of **Tanaghmelt**, which seemingly blends into the hillside; or for a longer walk 20km (12 miles) upstream to the Gorges of el-Abid, with about 15 smaller cascades, pools and beaches on the way. The charming **Riad Cascades d'Ouzoud** (www.ouzoud.com; *see page 135*) arranges longer treks in the area, as well as kayaking and abseiling in the dry canyons.

An extra attraction, particularly for children, are the large groups of Barbary apes who play and live around the falls, and who chase each other on the surrounding rocks, seemingly for the sole entertainment of tourists. Information signs advise you not to feed the animals, but sit down for lunch and they quickly venture towards the table to steal bread and whatever else they can grab.

The easiest way to get to the falls is by your own transport; otherwise take the bus from Marrakesh to Azilal and then a *grand taxi*. If you do have your own car, stop en route at **Demnate**, a lively walled town, with a wonderful **Sunday Souk**, famous for olives and local pottery.

Essaouira

The white and windy city of **Essaouira**, 175km (110 miles) west of Marrakesh, is one of the most attractive cities along Morocco's Atlantic coast. With its year-round mild temperatures, long history and leisurely pace it has always attracted artists and writers, and now also appeals to those escaping the Marrakesh buzz. The town can be visited on a day trip, but to do the place justice and to feel the full attraction, you need to stay at least one night. The old town has a few sights but the main pleasure is to stroll around the narrow streets,

Mending nets by the walls in Essaouira

explore the art galleries and colourful souks, watch the fishing boats come in, or sit on a café terrace to watch the comings and goings.

End the day on the rooftop of the Taros Café, just off the main square (2 rue de la Skala; daily 9am–midnight) to have a sundowner while you watch the sunset over the sea.

On the beach at Essaouira

Depending on who you ask, the name *Es-Saouir* has two extremely different meanings, either 'the little ramparts' or 'the beautifully designed'; but the town was also known in history as both Amougdoul and Mogador, names that probably go back to its Phoenician origins in the 7th century BC – *migdol* in Phoenician means lookout tower. The Phoenicians extracted the precious purple colour from the murex shells they found on the Île de Mogador, just off the mainland. The town as it looks today is entirely the work of Sultan Sidi Mohammed ben Abdallah, who in 1760 hired the Frenchman Théodore Cornut to design the city, and the walls, of his chosen naval basis.

The port kept growing in importance until the early 19th century, and the town amassed incredible wealth, mostly because of the role of the large Jewish community. There there were 17,000 Jews here, compared to fewer than 10,000 Muslims, and they had a special status as the middlemen between the Sultan and the foreign traders. Essaouira was the port for Timbuktu (now in Mali), and European goods such as Manchester cotton were exchanged here for African gold, salt, sugar, ivory and gum arabic.

By the 20th century the trade had dwindled, because the local Berber chieftains were more interested in arms deals and ransoms than in trading goods, and because most Jewish families had left. The French Protectorate chose Casablanca as its commercial centre. In the 1960s Essaouira became a favourite hippy hang-out, attracting musicians like Cat Stevens and Jimi Hendrix, as well as director Orson Welles, who shot his film *Othello* here. Then the surfers came, drawn by the huge waves and strong winds that give the town the title of 'Windy City of Africa'. In recent years they have been joined by throngs of house-buying Europeans.

The Medina and the Port

The picturesque old medina was declared a Unesco World Heritage site in 2001. The only way to explore the winding alleys of the medina is by foot and the best place to start is the picturesque place Moulay el-Hassan. The elegant square is now lined with café terraces, perfect for people-watching. On the south side of the square is a row of outdoor stalls, serving the freshest grilled fish and seafood, and announcing the entrance to the fishing port. The Porte de la Marine is part of the **Skala du Port** (daily 8.30am–noon and 2.30–6pm; charge), a sea bastion with cannons that protected the harbour. From the top there are superb views over the medina, the sea and the Île de Mogador, just offshore. This is a working harbour, which buzzes with activity all day long, with colourful fishing boats and an amazing variety of

Thuja wood

Essaouira is famous for its thuja woodwork, which comes from a thuja forest nearby, now under threat from a major tourist development south of the city. The *racines* (roots) of the tree provide a rich texture with knots, while the *tiges* (branches) give a lovely stripy pattern to dense chestnut-coloured wood.

The battlement-enclosed medina, Essaouira

fish for sale. Look out for the shipyard on the side where new boats are being built, and Chez Sam *(see page 142)*, a long-established fish restaurant at the end of the harbour from where you can watch all the activity.

Back on the square take the first street to the left, which skirts the city walls, towards the **Skala de la Ville**, an impressive 200m (655ft) sea bastion with 18th-century bronze cannons. The old ammunition warehouses underneath have been turned into workshops where the city's famous **thuja wood** is carved into boxes, salad bowls and furniture.

The rue Laalouj leads to the **Musée Sidi Mohammed ben Abdallah** (derb Laalouj; Wed–Mon 8.30am–6pm; charge) in the 19th-century town house of a pasha that was turned into the town hall during the French Protectorate. This small museum has a wonderful collection of the traditional crafts and decorative arts of the region. The ground floor focuses on antiquity, with Roman and Phoenician objects found in

The fishing harbour

the Bay of Essaouira, while the first floor is devoted to the inlaid woodwork and Arab and Jewish jewellery for which the city was renowned, as well as carpets and some delightful late 19th-century pictures of the city. One section has a fine collection of musical instruments, made in different local woods.

Mellah and Markets

Past the museum, at the crossroads, rue Sidi Mohammed ben Abdallah leads up to the narrow dark alleys of the old Jewish quarter (Mellah). Only three or four Jewish families still live here – many left for Israel long ago – and the area was falling apart until foreigners recently began buying houses.

From the **Bab Doukkala** at the end of the Mellah, the avenue Zerktouni, the city's main street, leads back to the harbour. On the right-hand side is the **Souk Jdid**, the main vegetable, fruit and fish markets, surrounded by spice shops.

On the opposite side of the road is the old **Marché de Grain** (Grain Market), which now has several pleasant cafés and some interesting shops. The street continues to the tree-lined **avenue Oqba ben Nafia**, the old *méchouar* (assembly place or processional avenue), with the splendid pink city walls. Several art galleries have opened, selling the colourful and primitive artwork of local Gnaoua artists *(see page 29)*. The first is Galerie d'Art Frederic Damgaard, which has the widest and most interesting collection.

Essaouira's wide sandy beach is a great place for a walk, but with regular gusts of strong wind it attracts more surfers, particularly kite surfers, than sunbathers. Like a mirage at the end of the beach appear the ruins of Borj el-Berod, an old fortress that is slowly disappearing in the sand. Locals are convinced that this was the inspiration for the Jimi Hendrix classic *Castles in the Sand*. Several outlets along the beach rent watersports equipment and offer courses. One of the most relaxed places to have lunch or hang out is the **Surf Club Océan Vagabond** (www.oceanvagabond.com).

If you are intrigued by the mysterious islands, formerly the Purple Islands and now the **Île de Mogador**, **Ciel et Mer** organises boat trips around them from the fishing harbour (two departures daily, four in summer). It's forbidden to go on land, as the islands are a nature reserve: a sanctuary for the protected Eleanora's falcons, who breed here between April and October before flying back to Madagascar.

The day's catch

WHAT TO DO

SHOPPING

Marrakesh is a shoppers' paradise: from strolling through the seemingly endless souks, haggling over Berber jewellery, couscous, spices or carpets, to browsing the trendy boutiques in Guéliz or the designer showrooms out in the Sidi Ghanem industrial zone, it has it all. Many of the shops in the souks sell similar wares, but venture off the well-trodden paths or check out the shops of new designers to find something different, chic or exotic. Many European designers have bought a house in the medina and been inspired by the city and its craftmanship, so you may find one of their creations waiting to be embroidered, or the prototype for next season's bag in one of the workshops. More often than not, local artisans will then produce a similar version at 'souk prices'. The more exclusive shops in the medina often work behind closed curtains for fear of their designs being copied. Marrakesh is now so established as a shopping destination that you can hire the services of personal shoppers, who will reveal all the city's secrets.

Crafts

Unlike many other places in the world, Marrakesh still produces many traditional crafts. With so many foreigners buying and decorating *riads*, not to mention the new influx of money that this brings, the crafts are flourishing. It is not surprising

Opening hours

The shops in the medina are usually open from 10am–8pm. Some close on Friday afternoon, and many are closed all day on Sunday. In Guéliz shops are open from Monday to Saturday 10am–1pm and again from 4–7.30pm.

Carpets are easily bagged

that so many designers flock to Marrakesh both for inspiration, and for craftsmen to realise their creations. It is said that if you can dream it up, someone somewhere in the medina can make it. Marrakesh is deservedly famous for its good-value leatherwork, from the traditional poufs and saddle bags to great travel bags and trendy sandals. Funky pottery is a good buy, as are wooden bowls – although many of those come from Essaouira.

A good place to start looking for traditional crafts is at the government-run **Ensemble Artisanal** *(see page 56)* on avenue Mohammed V opposite the Cyber Park. All kinds of craftsmen have a workshop here and sell their traditional wares at fixed prices. This is a good place to get an idea of what is available and what you can bargain for, before heading for the **souks**. The one-stop shop for furniture, lanterns, candlesticks, leather and pottery is **Mustapha Blaoui** at 144 rue Bab Doukkala. **Kifkif** at 3 rue des Ksour, Bab Laksour, does a modern take on local crafts. Several places in **Sidi Ghanem**, the industrial zone east of Marrakesh, make designer crafts that you can buy directly from the workshops.

Antiques and Carpets

Morocco has an endless variety of carpets and rugs in the most fabulous colours, changing from region to region. **Bazaar du Sud** at 117 in the **Souk des Tapis** has possibly the largest selection. In Guéliz, **Galerie Tadghart** at 11 Immeuble Berdai, on the corner of avenue Hassan I and the place de la Liberté has an exquisite collection of textiles. There are several **antique dealers** at the beginning of rue Dar el-Bacha and rue Sidi el-Yamani, but the most impressive, and one of the most well established, is **El-Badii** at 54 boulevard Moulay Rachid in Guéliz. The owner, Mr Bouskri, acts as a guide for distinguished visitors, and the museum-quality collection includes wonderful Berber jewelery, medieval manuscripts, textiles and carpets. For cheaper goods head to the souk outside **Bab el-Khemis**, which has most stalls on Thursday morning.

Art

Marrakesh has seen an explosion of arts in the last years and the opening of several galleries. Check out local listings for temporary exhibitions. **Ministerio de Gusto** at 22 Derb Azzouz in Mouassine is the home and avant-garde gallery of a former Italian fashion editor, with a good collection of works by contemporary artists in Marrakesh, including Hassan Hajjaj (www.hassanhajjaj.com) whose work is also available from the boutique at **Riad Yima**, 52B Derb Arjane Rakhba Kedima. **Gallerie 127** at 127 avenue Mohammed V displays contemporary photography. The **Matisse Gallery** on rue de Yougoslavie displays work by young Moroccan artists.

Ceramics are a special art

Babouches, Moroccan slippers

Jewellery

The best place to look for jewellery is in the souks, where you will find everything from tourist tat to antique, often Jewish-made, Berber jewellery. Near place des Ferblantiers is a covered **gold souk**, but the gold dowry jewellery is more likely to appeal to local women. For some unusual and good-value jewellery from Morocco and sub-Saharan Africa go to **Boutique Bel Hadj**, on the first floor of the Fondouk Ourzazi on the Bab Ftouh. The owner buys in some of the goods but also makes his own, and has a huge collection of beads.

Clothes

Behind the curtained windows of **Au Fil d'Or**, 10 Souk Semmarine, are fine kaftans, shirts and jackets in classic style for men and women. A made-to-measure service is on offer. For chic traditional women's clothes, styled for Western women and made to measure, there is no better and friendlier place than **Aya's** in Derb Jdid Bab Mellah, just off place des Ferblantiers. **La Maison du Kaftan**, 65 rue Sidi el-Yamami, may not look impressive at first but it has the widest selection of Moroccan clothing, including some velvet fabrics. Florence Taranne sells a chic and eclectic selection of African-Moroccan kaftans and accessories at **Kulchi**, 1 rue des Ksour. The most luxuriously embroidered kaftans and throws, all produced in India, are available from **Akbar Delights**, place Bab Ftouh, just off the Jemaa el-Fna.

Shoes and Leather

Follow the **Souk el-Kebir** and there is plenty of leather for sale: belts, suitcases, handbags and sandals. One piece of advice though: the leather weekend bags look great but sniff them before you buy, as it is very hard to get rid of the pungent smell. The **Souk des Babouches** has a great selection of the typical Moroccan slippers, which come in all colours, shapes and quality of leather. **I Love Marrakesh** in Souk Cherifia, Dar el-Bacha, is a new shop where French designer Laetitia Trouillet sells her funky locally-made handbags in a rainbow of bright colours.

In Guéliz the first stop for fine leather is 139 avenue Mohammed V where **Intensité Nomade** has international and local designer labels, and on the opposite corner, try **Place Vendome**. For Western-style shoes, the most popular place is **Atika** at 34 rue de la Liberté, or at 212 avenue Mohammed V.

Personal shopper

Apart from designing her delightful bags (see above) Laetitia Trouillet (tel. 074-217228; www.lalla.fr) also uses her inside knowledge of the souks and new town to work as the city's hippest personal shopper. She arranges a car, haggles and navigates her clients through the souks, so if you are looking for something in particular and have little time, she is your woman.

Morroco bound

Marrakesh, The Red City, The City Through Writers' Eyes Barnaby Rogerson and Stephen Lavington (eds) (Sickle Moon Books, London 2003)

Hideous Kinky by Esther Freud (Penguin, London 1992)

A Year in Marrakesh by Peter Mayne (Eland, London 2002)

The Voices of Marrakesh by Elias Canetti (Marian Boyars, London/New York 2001)

Lords of the Atlas, The Rise and Fall of Glaoua 1893–1956 by Gavin Maxwell (Century Publishing, London 1983)

Books

There are only a few bookshops in Marrakesh selling English-language books. The **Café du Livre**, at 44 rue Tarek Ibn Ziad in Guéliz, has become the favourite hangout for all anglophiles in town. Not only is this the best English-language bookshop in Marrakesh, with new books on Morocco as well as second-hand fiction, it is also the perfect place for a quiet coffee or delicious lunch while browsing a few choice volumes.

The best selection of beautiful coffee table books, not necessarily in English, is at **ACR Librairie d'Art** at the end of the passageway at 55 boulevard Zerktouni in Guéliz. **Librairie Chatr**, at 19–21 avenue Mohammed V, has a smaller selection of English paperbacks and trekking maps. In the medina there is a good bookstore with works on Moroccan arts and history in the courtyard of the **Musée de Marrakesh**.

NIGHTLIFE AND ENTERTAINMENT

Shopping may be exhausting, but keep a little breath for the city's increasingly varied nightlife. Hot new clubs and bars pop up all the time, mostly in the new town, but there are now quite a few in the medina too. The best place to start the evening is on the **Jemaa el-Fna** which has food, music and entertainers *(see pages 26–9)*.

Bars

The coolest place to hang out in the medina is the **Terrace des Epices** (Souk Cherifia, rue Dar el-Bacha), open during the day and at night, with a relaxed atmosphere and peaceful views over the rooftops. Also in the medina is the **Kosybar** (place des Ferblantiers), which combines three different venues in one *riad*: a Moroccan tea salon, a sushi bar and a rooftop lounge bar. The meeting place in the new town is the colonial-style **Grand Café de la Poste** just behind the main post office on avenue Mohammed V, with a large outdoor terrace. Much talked-about bar-restaurant **Villa Rosa** (64 avenue Hassan II, Guéliz; tel: 024-449635) is one of the places to meet for a drink before moving on to dinner next door. **Le Comptoir** (rue Ech-chouhada, Hivernage; tel: 024-437702; www.ilove-marrakesh.com/lecomptoir), a sister venue of the Comptoir Paris, is a popular place to end, with a nightly belly dancing show.

Musicians at Le Comptoir restaurant and club

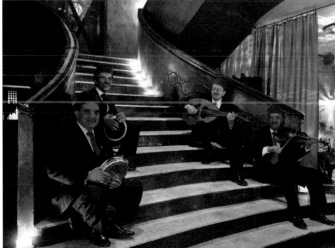

Nightclubs

Marrakesh no longer goes to bed early, and with the arrival of Pacha, the city is acquiring an Ibiza-like reputation for nightlife. Most of the clubs are in Guéliz and Hivernage. **Pacha Marrakesh** (boulevard Mohammed VI; tel: 024-388405; www.pachamarrakech.com) is a large entertainment complex with several restaurants, lounges and a large clubbing area where the world's best DJs turn the tables. The old theatre at the Saadi hotel has been converted into the high-end club **Teatro** (Hotel es Saadi, Hivernage). **Jad Mahal** (10 rue Haroun er-Rachid, Hivernage; tel: 024-436984) has underground club nights and regular live music sessions. Set in an old villa is **Montecristo** (20 rue Ibn Aicha, Guéliz; tel: 024-439031), which has several floors of music and dancing, and a rooftop where you can try a typical Moroccan waterpipe. The **Suite Club** (Hotel Le Méridien N'Fis, avenue Mohammed V; tel: 024-420700; www.suiteclub.ma) attracts an international crowd.

Cultural Life

Most of the films screened in Marrakesh are in French or Arabic, and foreign films are often dubbed. The best cinemas in town are **Le Colisée** (boulevard Mohammed Zerktouni, Guéliz) and **Mégarama** (boulevard Mohammed VI, behind Pacha; tel: 024-386865). The **Institut Français** (Route de Targa; tel: 024-446930) shows arthouse French and North African films.

For a more exotic experience, where the audience is often more entertaining than the film, head for the Cinema Eden (Derb Debbachi, off the Jemaa el-Fna), which was depicted by Spanish writer Juan Goytisolo in his book *Cinema Eden: Essays from the Muslim Mediteranean*. The Théâtre Royal (avenue de France; tel: 024-431516; *see page 57*) only stages occasional performances, but is worth checking out.

HAMMAMS AND SPAS

One of the best ways to relax is to go to a traditional *hammam* (Turkish bath). The **Hammam el-Bacha** (20 rue Fatima Zohra) in the medina has seperate times for men and women. For a more upmarket experience try the *hammam* at **La Maison Arabe** (1 Derb Assebhe, Bab Doukkala; tel: 024-387010; www.lamaisonarabe) or **Les Bains de Marrakesh** (2 Derb Sedra, Bab Agnaou; www.lesbainsdemarrakech.com). Several *riads* and hotels offer spa facilities, but some of the best are at the new **Angsana Riad** (tel: 024-421979; www.angsana.com) and at the **Beldi Country Club** (tel. 024-383950). For the most indulgent *hammam* go to **Palais Rhoul and Spa** in the Palmeraie (tel: 024-329494/95; www.palais rhoul.com) where the *hammamiste* will scrub you, throw buckets of water, give you a massage and finish off by squeezing an orange over you.

Pamper yourself in a candlelit bathroom

SPORTS

In addition to its exciting nightlife and fantastic shopping, Marrakesh caters for sports enthusiasts and those who just want to escape the city for some fresh country air.

Swimming and Beaches

The little dip pools in the *riads* are good to cool off after a hot day but not satisfying for those who want to swim or have a day by the pool. Some hotels with larger pools let you use the pool if you have lunch, including **El Andalous** (avenue du Président Kennedy, Hivernage; tel: 024-448226) and the **Jnane Tamsna** (Palmeraie; tel: 024-329423; www.jnane tamsna.com). **Nikki Beach** (Circuit de la Palmeraie; tel: 063-519992; www.nikkibeach.com) of St Tropez and Miami fame have opened their doors to a day-long-party-by-the-pool experience, but be sure to bring your most fashionable swimwear. Few people realise that **Pacha** *(see page 88)* has a lovely pool with a restaurant for use during the day; and the **Beldi Country Club** *(see page 65)* has two pools set in a large rose garden. **Lake Lalla Takerkoust** near Marrakesh *(see page 67)* is a more natural option.

Cycling

As Marrakesh is relatively small it is easy to get around town on a bike. In Guéliz the **Hotel Toulousain** (rue Tarek ibn Ziad; tel: 024-430033; www.geocities.com/hotel_toulousain) rents bikes by the day. **Actions & Loisirs** (1 avenue Yaqoub el-Mansour, Guéliz; tel: 024-430931) has a wider selection, more appropriate for getting further out of town.

Horse Riding

There are several good stables near Marrakesh. The **Cavaliers de l'Atlas** (tel: 061-464327; www.lescavaliersdelatlas.

com) and the **Club Equestre de la Palmeraie Golf Palace** (Circuit de la Palmeraie, tel: 024-301010; www.pgp.co.ma) have horses and ponies most suitable for children. Nearby is the **Club Equestre de la Palmeraie** (tel: 024-329451), also located in the palm groves.

Trekking and Running

Plenty of people go jogging in the Palmeraie, but more serious runners could join the annual **Marrakesh Marathon** (www.runningclubmaroc.com). Trekking options abound in all directions outside Marrakesh. The eco-lodge **Kasbah du Toubkal** *(see page 71)*, with stunning views, is a popular destination for an easy mountain walk combined with lunch. Other destinations are the idyllic **Cascades d'Ouzoud** *(see pages 72–3)*, the artificial **Lake Lalla Takerkoust** *(see page 67)* and the popular **Ourika Valley** *(see page 68)*.

On horseback up Mount Toubkal

The Royal Golf Club

Golf
There are three golf courses in town: the **Club de la Palmeraie Golf Palace** (tel: 024-301010; www.pgp.co.ma), **Golf d'Amelkis** (tel: 024-449288) and the **Royal Golf Club** (tel: 024-404705), which all have 18 holes. The latter is the oldest golf club in Morocco, opened by the Pasha of Marrakesh in 1923. **Fédération Royale Marocaine de Golf** (tel: 037-755960) can provide information on tournaments.

Ballooning
You will need a clear winter's day for full effect, but a bird's-eye view of the 'Red City', the surrounding palm groves and the snow-clad Atlas could prove the most memorable part of your stay. The flights offered by **Ciel d'Afrique** (15 rue Mauritania, Guéliz; tel: 024-432843) cost slightly more than Dh2000 per person (half-price for children under 10), plus extra for breakfast and champagne.

CHILDREN'S MARRAKESH

Moroccans love children and most children love Morocco. Check when booking a *riad* that the place is safe for children. Unless you rent the whole house, *riads* are not recommended for small children, as noise echoes through the courtyards. Many restaurants cater for the clubbing crowds so find a family-friendly one like Chez Chegrouni *(see page 137)*, Catanzaro *(see page 139)*, or the stalls at Jemaa el-Fna. Children will love the large selection of excellent ice creams at **Oliveri** *(see page 140)*, a Marrakchi institution.

Watching snake charmers, acrobats and musicians in the **Jemaa el-Fna** is fascinating, but avoid the henna tattoos as the chemicals can provoke an allergic reaction. Kids love walking in the **souks** buying little souvenirs, and holding the **chameleons** in the spice shops of the Rakhba Kedima.

Choosing a hotel with a **swimming pool** is a good way to keep children entertained in the heat of the day, but there are plenty of swimming options *(see page 90)* if you are staying in a *riad*. **Oasiria** (4km along Route du Barrage; tel: 024-380438; www.ilove-marrakesh.com/oasiria; summer daily 10am–6pm; charge, free shuttle bus from Marrakesh) is a large water park with all the usual facilities. Horse riding *(see page 90)* is a fine way to end the afternoon, as is the **Jnane el-Harti** *(see page 57)* which has a children's play area. At the **Tansift Garden** in the Palmeraie (daily 8am–10pm) children can ride on a camel – or a dromedary, to be precise.

Take a ride in a calèche

Calendar of Events

Every night is a party in Jemaa el-Fna (see page 26), but since King Mohammed VI ascended to the throne, he has been keen on promoting the city's many different assets through a variety of festivals. The dates of these festivals vary, and they are usually held in various locations in the medina. The best place to find information is online or at the Tourist Office (see page 127).

The month of Ramadan is a special time to be in the medina. It is the Muslim month of fasting, when local people abstain from food, drink, smoking and sex from sunrise to sunset. Many restaurants and bars are shut during the day, but at night the city celebrates. The whole town seems to come to Jemaa el-Fna square to eat and watch the performers. At the end of Ramadan is the Eid al-Fitr, when for two days families get together and eat. Islamic holidays are based on the lunar calendar and occur 11 days earlier each year.

January: *The Marrakesh Marathon* (www.marathon-marrakech.com) is run by more than 5,000 Moroccan and foreign athletes through the medina and the Palmeraie.

February: *Dakka Marrakchia Festival* is the annual festival of traditional music in several locations in the medina.

April: *Jardin'Art* (www.jardinsdumaroc.com/festival) is a celebration of Moroccan traditional and contemporary gardens in several locations.

June: *Marrakesh Popular Arts Festival* (www.marrakechfestival.com) is a week-long bonanza of music, arts, folklore and a nightly fantasia (show on horseback). Later in the month is the now well-established *Festival d'Essaouira* (www.festival-gnaoua.net), a world music event that attracts performers from around the globe and more than 200,000 partygoers.

August: *The Moussem of Setti Fatma* celebrates the local saint after which the village in the Ourika was named. There is a large market and musical performances.

November–December: *Marrakesh International Film Festival* (www.festival-marrakech.com), King Mohammed VI's favourite festival, attended by many Hollywood stars.

EATING OUT

In a Moroccan home, cooking is traditionally women's business – the men are only allowed to make tea. Wealthy families are devoted to their female *dada*, often a descendant from African slaves, who cooks marvellous meals and looks after the children. In other families the art is passed on from mother to daughter. To sample the best Moroccan food you need to be lucky enough to get invited to someone's home. Moroccan dishes take hours to prepare, so in restaurants, the food – cooked mostly by male chefs – is often prepared a long time in advance and reheated. Remember that many specialities, such as couscous or roast shoulder of lamb, need to be ordered 24 hours in advance.

Dining out in style

Restaurants

In Marrakesh, as everywhere else, the wise advice is to eat where local people eat: except that here, while the locals don't mind a quick bite of Moroccan street food, when it comes to eating properly the only place to eat Moroccan cuisine is at home. If they do go out to a restaurant, it is usually to eat French, Italian or Japanese food, or to a place that combines drinks with morsels to eat. When asked which is the best Moroccan restaurant in the medina, you may be hard pressed to find a local person who has been to any of them.

Several *riads* in the medina, like Stylia, Yaqout or Dar Moha, offer gourmet set menus, including several salads, a soup, a pastilla, couscous or *tagine* (stew) and dessert, which come with magnificent exotic surroundings, luxurious seating and classical Moorish music. The food is good, albeit expensive by Moroccan standards, but most people can only do it once – the majority find it hard to get beyond the third course. Failing an invitation to a private home, order dinner in your *riad*: this will be the closest you get to home cooking.

Almost every week another restaurant opens its doors in Marrakesh, with a new concept, an even trendier setting and a more 'fusioned' menu. Consistency is a problem, as the

Lamb, the traditional meat, is cooked with potatoes and peas

restless crowds of Marrakchis and expats move from new place to newer, and the chefs come and go. It is no secret that restaurant and *riad* owners often snatch staff from their competitors while out for dinner. In recent years the selection of restaurants has become very cosmopolitan with every cuisine represented from the very popular Mediterranean dishes to the increasingly sought-after Japanese sushi and sashimi.

Cookery classes

Many *riad* hotels organise cookery classes where you can accompany the house chef to the local market and learn how to cook *tagines* or couscous. More elaborate classes are available from **Souk Cuisine** (tel: 073-804955; www.soukcuisine.com), which organises culinary weeks in Marrakesh; **La Maison Arabe** (tel: 024-387010; www.lamaison arabe.com); and, in the Palmeraie, the **Jnane Tamsna** (tel: 024-329423; www.jnanetamsna.com).

Meal Times

Breakfast is usually served around 8 or 9am and is either a French-style meal of *café au lait* (milky coffee), baguette and croissant, or a delicious Moroccan-style spread with flat Moroccan bread (*khubz*), *amlou* (paste of crushed almonds with honey and argan oil), *beghrir* (a Moroccan pancake version of crumpets) with jam or honey, and freshly baked *rghaif* (flat buttery layered pastry). All usually come with freshly squeezed orange juice. **Lunch** is traditionally the most important meal in the day, and is eaten at any time between 1 and 4pm, when most shops and offices are closed. Lunch usually means a selection of salads and vegetable dishes, followed by a main course of couscous, *tagine* or *mechoui* (roast lamb) followed by a much needed mint tea, sweets and most probably a little nap. If you are in a hurry, there are plenty of faster options including *brochettes*, *merguez*, sandwiches and quick-fix *tagines*.

Dinner is eaten after the sunset *passeggiata* (evening stroll), from 9pm onwards. Most people eat a soup or lunch left-overs at home, but in Marrakesh families head to the 'Place', Jemaa el-Fna, for a snack, while young people go out for a pizza or a bite with drinks.

Local Specialities

Among the many culinary delights Marrakesh has to offer, don't leave without sampling the following regional favourites.

Bread

Bread, either the French baguette or Moroccan flat bread, is eaten with every meal. It is always bought fresh from the local *hanout* or corner shop just before the meal. Often it is used instead of cutlery to scoop up vegetables or meat. Never take more bread than you need: Moroccans hold it in high regard as a 'gift from God', so it should never be wasted.

Ramadan

Most Moroccans don't eat or drink from sunrise to sunset during the Holy Month of Ramadan. They break the fast with the meal called *iftour*, have dinner later in the evening, and eat breakfast before the sun comes up. Many restaurants close for the month or only open for *iftour* with a special Ramadan menu, but in hotels and the more touristic areas of Marrakesh many places remain open all day. Tourists are not expected to fast, but they should eat and drink out of public view.

Couscous

Couscous is the national dish of Morocco, Algeria, Tunisia and Libya. The name comes from the Berber word *seksou*, and it consists of small grains of semolina.

In the West the fast-food pre-cooked version of couscous is most commonly found: you just need to add boiling water to the dry semolina and let it soak for a few minutes until it is

Mealtime on the Jemaa el-Fna

ready. In North Africa women traditionally make their own couscous by rolling two parts of semolina with one part of flour, some salted water and a little oil, until it is grain-sized. Once a batch is made it can be stored for a while.

Couscous is steamed above a reduced broth of meat, vegetables and spices, with which it is then served. It can be served with fish, as in Essaouira, or with just vegetables. The best couscous is cooked at home, or ordered in advance in a restaurant.

Diffa

The *diffa*, or Moroccan feast in someone's home or at a medina palace restaurant, consists of numerous courses. It starts with a selection of *mezze* or salads – between four and 10, mostly vegetables and dips eaten with bread, and *briouates*, tiny fried filo pastries stuffed with meat, cheese or spinach.

The traditional Moroccan soup is *harira*, made with lamb broth, tomatoes, chickpeas and lots of spices. It is a hearty soup often served with a few dates on the side. (In Ramadan, the month of fasting, *harira* and dates are served at sundown to break the fast). Instead of soup – or after it – there is often *b'stilla*, a delicious 'pie' with layers of *warka* (fine filo pastry) and pigeon or chicken cooked with caramelised onion and toasted almonds, then dusted with icing sugar and cinnamon. The lighter version of *b'stilla* comes with seafood instead of meat. The main course is *couscous* with meat and/or the traditional *sept légumes* (seven vegetables), a choice of *tagines* (meat, chicken or fish stews, often cooked with some sort of fruit) or a *mechoui* (slow roasted lamb or goat). The traditional *mechoui*, a whole lamb or kid slow roasted in a clay oven, is often served for special occasions, like weddings. Fish is delicious in Morocco but is not often on the menu in Marrakesh.

Dessert

Dessert in Morocco is often fresh fruit, particularly melon, watermelon or slices of orange sprinkled with cinnamon. Sweet *pastilla au lait* consists of layers of *warka* (filo pastry)

Mint and Chinese Gunpowder Tea

Moroccan mint (*Mentha piperita*), a fragrant kind of peppermint, is indigenous to Morocco. When in 1720 England's King George I offered the Sultan of Morocco a box of Chinese green tea as a gift, it was considered too pungent and bitter to drink neat, so the Moroccans mixed it with the sugar and mint widely available in the local markets. These days the tea is still made with Gunpowder tea, an inexpensive Chinese green tea which was originally rolled to preserve its freshness for the long journey from China to Africa. Mint tea has become the national drink of Morocco, and according to the Moroccan trade ministry, the country is the major importer of Chinese green tea worldwide.

Tagines, the traditional cookware

filled with a light orange blossom-flavoured crème anglaise or custard and nuts. Mint tea is served with a selection of sweet pastries made with almonds, nuts or honey. The finest is the *Kaab el-ghzal* or *corne de gazelle* (gazelle's horn), a crusty pastry in a horn shape stuffed with almond paste perfumed with orange blossom. *Shebbakia* are fried pastries which are dipped in hot honey and sesame seeds, served during Ramadan.

Traditional Dishes

bessara a thick soup of fava beans, olive oil and spices.
couscous perhaps Morocco's most famous dish. Of Berber origin, it is steamed semolina served with a broth of meat and vegetables – traditionally seven different ones.
harira rich lamb and chickpea soup eaten with dates.
loobia bean stew.
merguez hot spicy lamb sausages.

Dried fruits and nuts

pastilla a multi-layered filo pastry with delicately sweetened pigeon.

ras el-hanout a mixture of 27 spices used on special occasions, particularly in stews.

tajine stew of meat or fish with fruit or vegetables, eaten with bread, cooked in the typical conical earthenware pot. The most traditional is *tajine mqalli*: chicken with olives and preserved lemon.

tanjia Marrakchi slow-cooked lamb stew cooked in an urn-shaped earthenware crockpot.

Drinks

Water and a variety of fizzy drinks are available everywhere, and are usually much cheaper than in Europe. In many places in Marrakesh you can find delicious fresh juices; depending on the time of year they may include orange juice (plentiful on the Jemaa el-Fna), banana, avocado and carrot juice, and *lait d'amande* (almond milk). Make sure the juice is squeezed in front of you, and that the vendor doesn't add tap water.

Alcohol is forbidden by the Koran, so in theory Muslims do not drink it, although a lot of Marrakchis do. Many Moroccan restaurants don't serve alcohol, but most of those in Marrakesh do. In our listings *(see pages 136–42)* we have noted those that are no-alcohol zones. The local beer is Flag, or the slightly more expensive, locally brewed Heineken and Casablanca, sold in beautiful bottles. In up-market establishments foreign beers are also available. Since Roman times most of the local wines have been produced in Meknes, and plenty are very drinkable. The best reds are Cuvée du President, Médaillon, Domaine de Sahari, Ksar, Guerrouane and Siroua. Good whites are Val d'Argan, Valpierre and Chaud-Soleil, while among the rosés the Preesident and Guerrouane are most recommended. The renowned French wine makers Châteauneuf du Pape are now producing a very good wine near Essaouira – the Val d'Argan red, rosé and white. For something typically Moroccan, *mahia* is a strong fig liqueur sometimes served as a *digestif*.

Moroccan coffee comes very strong and black; if you want it with milk ask for a *noss noss* or a *café au lait*. If you want milk with some coffee in it, ask for a *café cassé*. The most popular drink at any time of the day or night is *thé à la menthe*, or green tea with mint. Sometimes in winter the tea is served with *chiba* (absinthe) or *fliou* (menthol), and special guests are treated to mint tea with almonds or pine nuts.

Time for tea

To Help You Order...

Do you have a table?	**Avez-vous une table?**
I would like to book a table please	**Je voudrais réserver une table s'il vous plaît**
I'd like a/an/some...	**Je voudrais...**
The bill, please	**L'addition s'il vous plaît**
I'm a vegetarian	**Je suis végétarien, je ne mange pas la viande**
breakfast	**le petit déjeuner**
lunch	**le déjeuner**
dinner	**le dîner**
This is delicious	**C'est délicieux**

...and Read the Menu

fresh orange juice	**orange pressé**	brochettes	**kebabs**
(mineral) water	**de l'eau (minérale)**	fish	**poisson**
white coffee	**café au lait/ café crème/ noss noss**	prawns	**crevettes**
		squid	**calamar**
		vegetables	**légumes**
		fruit	**fruit**
mint tea	**thé à la menthe**	beans	**haricots**
		garlic	**ail**
black tea	**thé noir**	potatoes	**pommes de terre**
beer	**bière**	pumpkin	**potiron**
wine	**vin**	apple	**pomme**
salt	**sel**	dates	**dattes**
pepper	**poivre**	grapes	**raisins**
meat	**viande**	lemon	**citron**
beef	**boeuf**	watermelon	**pastèque**
lamb	**agneau**	pomegranate	**grenade**
chicken	**poulet**	cactus fruit	**figue de Barbarie**
liver	**foie**		

HANDY TRAVEL TIPS

An A–Z Summary of Practical Information

A

ACCOMMODATION

Marrakesh has an incredible range of accommodation, running the gamut from the celebrated luxury hotels such as the Mamounia and the Saadi, both of which have been renovated to shiny new splendour, to the legendary fleapits like the Essaouira and Le Foucault; from the magnificent palace in the medina to the atmospheric backpackers' hangout and everything in between.

The converted courtyard houses known as *riads* offer some of the city's most charming accommodation. A good place to look is www.boutiquesouk.com, a very successful concierge service in Marrakesh, which not only has a great portfolio of *riads* and hotels, but also a husband and wife team who advise on the hippest places and parties in town. The new and upcoming company Villanovo (www.villanovo.com) specialises in charming and characterful accommodation, mostly in Marrakesh but also Casablanca and Essaouira. The website www.hipmarrakesh.com lists English-speaking *riads* in town.

Most tourists arriving on a package tour stay in a resort hotel on the outskirts of town, while the majority of individual travellers head for a *riad* in the medina. A *riad* is a traditional house in the medina built around a garden courtyard. Most local people have moved out of the medina and their houses have been bought by foreigners. The *riads* were renovated and converted into *maisons d'hôte* (the French term for guest house) but are more like small boutique hotels. Most *riads* are in the mid-range bracket, with the exception of a few remaining budget places and a now increasing number of luxury hotels – the latest being the Banyan chain which runs the Angsana Hotel. The advantage of the *riads* is that they are right in the medina. It is like staying in a friendly home, and if you don't feel like going out you can order delicious home-cooked food. Some visitors, however, having booked a week or two-week stay, can feel claustrophobic after a few days and long to be somewhere more open and spacious. The ideal arrangement for a week in Marrakesh would be to book a few days in a *riad* in the medina and a few days in the Palmeraie or on the outskirts of town, where you can enjoy nature, peace and quiet, and a swimming pool.

Most three-, four- and five-star hotels in Guéliz and Hivernage offer better value than the medina lodgings, and have the added advantage of being near the restaurants, trendy shopping and nightlife. Hotels in the Palmeraie tend to offer extreme luxury, are far away from the action and perfect for hanging out by the pool after a few days of shopping in the souks.

Many hotels have high and low season prices: high season is mostly February–May and September–October, as well as Christmas and New Year.

Do you have a single/double room?	**Avez-vous une chambre pour une personne/double?**
with bath/shower	**avec bain/douche**
with double bed/twin beds	**avec un double lit/deux lits**
What's the rate per night?	**C'est combien la nuit?**

AIRPORT

Marrakesh's Menara Airport is 5km (3 miles) southwest of town. The arrivals hall has banks, exchange booths, ATMs and car rental agencies. The number 11 bus runs every half an hour from the airport to the Jemaa el-Fna. The number L19 bus runs hourly from 7am–midnight from the airport to Guéliz. The fare is currently Dh20 one way, or Dh30 for the round trip, and the ticket is valid for two weeks.

The easiest way to get into town is by *petit taxi* (meter taxi for a maximum of three passengers); they park outside the terminal. There is a fixed fare of Dh50 (day) or Dh80 (night) to the Jemaa el-Fna, Dh60/90 to Guéliz and Dh100–150 to the Palmeraie. *Grands taxis* or shared taxis that will take up to six passengers have a fixed price of around Dh70 to the Jemaa el-Fna or Guéliz – there are prices posted on the notice board.

If it is the first time you have visited a particular *riad* or hotel in the medina or the Palmeraie, ask the hotel for a transfer, as the taxi driver may have trouble finding the place in the maze of the medina's alleys or the *pistes* in the Palmeraie. Prices for transfers are usually quite reasonable.

Where can I get a taxi?	**Oú est-ce que je peux trouver un taxi?**
How much is it to the Jemaa el-Fna?	**Combien ça coute pour aller à la Jemaa el-Fna?**
Does this bus go to?	**Est-ce que ce bus va jusqu' à ...?**

B

BICYCLE HIRE

If you are reasonably fit, a bike is a fun way to get around the medina and the *ville nouvelle*, and it avoids haggling with taxi drivers. Some of the most popular cycling routes take in a ride around Marrakesh's city walls or go through gardens such as the Palmeraie, the Menara and Agdal.

Bicycle rental is readily available from many budget hotels in the medina or in Guéliz, including Hotel Toulousain (44 rue Tareq ibn Ziad, Guéliz; tel: 024-430033) Prices are currently (2008) Dh80 for a day and Dh50 for a half-day *(see page 90)*.

BUDGETING FOR YOUR TRIP

Life in Morocco is cheaper than in most European countries, but prices in Marrakesh tend to be higher than elsewhere in the country. Prices quoted are correct in 2008 but are only approximate.

Accommodation. A double room in a *riad* in the medina starts at Dh500 (£35/$70), mid-range is about Dh1,200 (£85/$170) and quickly soars to over Dh2,500 (£175/$350), including all taxes and breakfast.

Airport transfer. The shuttle bus from the airport to the medina and Guéliz costs Dh20 (£1.40/$2.80) one way, or Dh30 (£2.10/$4.20) for the round trip, with the ticket valid for two weeks. A *petit taxi* (meter taxi for maximum three passengers) from outside the terminal costs Dh50 (£3.50/$7), Dh80 (£5.60/$11.20) at night, to the Jemaa el-Fna; Dh60 (£4.20/$8.40), Dh90 (£6.30/$12.60) at night, to Guéliz; and Dh100–150 (£7–10.50/$14–21) to the Palmeraie.

Car hire. Car hire is relatively expensive and it pays to shop around. Prices for a compact car with manual transmission, mandatory liability insurance, unlimited mileage but without air-conditioning will cost from Dh600 (£40/$80) a day, but is slightly cheaper when you rent for a week. Fuel currently costs around Dh9 (£0.65/$1.25) per litre.

Entertainment. Nightclubs and discos are usually free if you buy drinks or dinner; if there is a charge it is around Dh150 (£10.50/$21) on weekday after 10pm, and Dh300 (£21/$42) at weekends. Drinks are from Dh40 (£2.80/$5.60).

Flights. A flight from London to Marrakesh will cost around £200/$400.

Local transport. It is easy to get around town on foot; a taxi ride from Gueliz to the Jemaa el-Fna will cost on average around Dh20 (£1.40/$2.80).

Meals. A meal in a cheap restaurant will cost on average between Dh30–50 (£2.10–3.50/$4.20–7) per person. A three-course meal in a mid-range restaurant will cost around Dh200 (£14/$28) per person without alcoholic drinks, while up-market restaurants start at around Dh300 per person (£21/$42).

Sightseeing. The entrance fee to most sights is Dh15/20 (£1–1.40/$2–2.80).

C

CAMPING

There are two camping sites, but they are both a fair distance out of town. **Camping-Caravaning Ferdaous** (11km/7 miles out of town on the Casablanca Road; tel: 024-304090/061-552843) is beside the highway and therefore quite noisy, and there is no public transport, but it is shady and the facilities are clean. **Camping Le Relais de Marrakesh** (10km/6 miles on the Marrakesh Road; tel: 024-302103; www.lerelaisdemarrakech.com) has a swimming pool and is clean.

CAR HIRE *(Voiture de location)* (See also DRIVING)

You don't need a car to get around Marrakesh; it is easier to walk or take a *petit taxi* for longer distances, but to see the surrounding area it is worth having your own transport. Most of the international car rental agencies, such as Hertz, Avis, Budget and Europcar, have offices at Marrakesh airport and in town, but local agencies are often cheaper. Many companies offer discounts of up to 30 percent if you book in advance over the internet, but do shop around, as prices vary quite a lot.

Prices for a compact car with manual transmission, mandatory liability insurance and unlimited mileage but without air-conditioning start at Dh600 a day, but are slightly cheaper when you rent for a week. Most agencies will either ask for a (returnable) cash deposit (around Dh3,000–5,000) or will take an impression of your credit card.

The minimum age for driving is 18, but most car rental companies require drivers to be at least 21. You must carry your driving licence, international or EU, and passport at all times.

Read your rental agreement carefully. Most contracts don't cover you for off-road driving, so you are not covered for damages or if you break down on *pistes*.

I'd like to rent a car.	J'aimerai louer une voiture.
tomorrow	demain
for one day/week	pour un jour, pour la semaine
Is insurance included?	Est-ce que l'assurance est inclus?
unlimited mileage	kilométrage illimité

CLIMATE

Marrakesh has mild winters and very hot summers. The best times to visit are in spring and autumn, when the temperatures are around 20 to 25°C (68–77°F), and around 10°C (50°F) at night. From November to March it may be sunny during the day but it gets cold at night, so make sure to book accommodation with heating. This is also the time for occasional rainfall. There is the chance of a desert storm in April, and a hot desert wind blows in June. In the summer it gets really hot, often in the high 30s or over 40°C (104°F). In summer many Marrakchis head for the coast or the mountains.

	J	F	M	A	M	J	J	A	S	O	N	D
°C	18	19	22	23	27	31	36	36	32	27	22	19
°F	64	66	72	73	81	88	97	97	90	81	72	66

CLOTHING (Vêtements)

You never really have to dress warmly in Marrakesh; just bring a sweater or warm shawl for cold winter nights. In spring bring a warm fleece and a rain jacket, but most of the time light clothes will be fine. A folding umbrella can be really useful, too. In autumn bring a sweater or light jacket and loose cotton clothing. Summer is very hot, so stick to light cotton clothing, swimwear for the pool and a sun hat. During the day the dress code is very relaxed but at night people dress up to go out to the trendier restaurants and bars – hippy chic is the trend of the moment.

Many Moroccan women still wear a long kaftan with sleeves when they go out, so if you don't want to stand out too much, and in order to respect local customs, women should avoid going to the souks or wandering around the medina in skimpy shorts or see-through clothing. Men should refrain from removing their shirts in town, however hot it may be.

CRIME AND SAFETY (See also EMERGENCIES and POLICE)

Marrakesh is traditionally safer than most European cities, but visitors should still take the usual precautions. Women should make sure their handbags are closed, and slung across their shoulders, and everyone should carry valuables and wallets in inside pockets. Do not produce large sums of money when you are making a purchase. Watch out for pickpockets in crowded places, particularly the Jemaa el-Fna and the souks. Muggings are pretty rare. As so many people now stay in the medina, it has become safer to walk there at night, although some of the *riads* now pay for extra security near the entrances to the medina.

Morocco is the world's largest cannabis producer. Moderate local use is tolerated by the police, but the sale and consumption of drugs is strictly illegal.

CUSTOMS AND ENTRY REQUIREMENTS

A current passport is required for entry to Morocco, and it must be valid for at least six months after the date of entry. Visas are not required for visits lasting under three months for EU, USA, Canadian, Australian and New Zealand citizens, but South Africans must apply for a visa at the Moroccan embassy in Pretoria.

Currency restrictions. Visitors can carry unlimited amounts of foreign currency in and out of the country, but all amounts exceeding Dh15,000 in foreign currency must be declared.

Customs. Visitors can bring in 1 litre of liquor, 1 litre of wine, 200 cigarettes or 50 cigars, and 5g of perfume duty-free.

D

DRIVING (see also CAR RENTAL)

You can drive in Marrakesh, but traffic is becoming an issue. Most of the medina is pedestrianised so a car is not needed there. For most visitors a private taxi will be an easier way to navigate the city. Parking spaces are scarce, and the parking zones are watched by *gardiens de voitures* (parking attendants) in blue coats. They will more or less watch the car for you, and the going rate is about Dh10 for a few hours and Dh20–30 for overnight. In Guéliz there are now more and more parking meters.

You only really need a car if you are going to explore the countryside. As you leave Marrakesh there are Gendarmerie Royale checkpoints on the outskirts of town, and although foreigners are not usually stopped, it is advisable to slow down and say hello. Watch the signs for speed limits when driving out of the city as the likelihood of a policeman or a radar check is very high, and fines have to be paid on the spot. Always carry your passport and registration or car-rental documents with you. The roads are in quite good condition as you drive out of Marrakesh.

Driving is on the right, and seatbelts are compulsory. During the day the traffic can be chaotic but it is quite slow-moving. Avoid driving at night, if possible, as it can be dangerous.

Are we on the right road for...?	**Est-ce que nous sommes sur le bon chemin pour...?**
É esta estrada para...?	**Est-ce que cette rue mène à...**
Fill the tank, please with... three star/four star diesel	**Le plein s'il-vous plaît, avec normal/super gazole**
My car's broken down.	**Ma voiture est en panne**
I have a flat tyre	**J'ai un pneu crevé**

E

ELECTRICITY

Morocco operates on 220V AC/50Hz. Plugs are of the European two-pin variety. Visitors from the USA will need a transformer to use their own appliances.

I need an adaptor/ battery, please.	**J'ai besoin d'un adapteur/ d'une pile électrique s'il vous plaît.**

EMBASSIES AND CONSULATES

In Morocco

Most embassies and consulates are in Rabat. In Marrakesh there is a **British Honorary Consul** (Résidence Taib, 55 boulevard Mohammed Zerktouni, Guéliz; tel: 044-436078), and the **Honorary Consul of Ireland** is in Casablanca (tel: 022-660306). **Australia** does not have a consulate or embassy in Morocco. Consular assistance is provided by the Canadian Embassy.

Canadian Embassy: 13 bis rue Jaafa as-Sadiq, Agdal, Rabat; tel: 037-687400; fax: 037-687430; www.rabat.gc.ca.

South African Embassy: 34 rue des Saadiens, Rabat; tel: 037-706760; fax: 037-724550.

UK Embassy: 28 avenue S.A.R. Sidi Mohammed, Souissi, Rabat; tel: 037-633333; www.britishembassy.gov.uk/morocco.

US Embassy: 2 avenue Mohammed el-Fassi, Rabat; tel: 037-762265; fax: 037-765661; www.usembassy.ma.

Moroccan Diplomatic Missions Abroad

Australia: There is no Moroccan consulate or embassy in Australia. Consular assistance to Australian citizens in Morocco is provided by the Moroccan Consulate in Paris, 12 rue de la Saida, 75015 Paris; tel: 01-5656 7200.

Canada: Moroccan Embassy, 38 Range Road, Ottawa, Ontario K1N 8J4; tel: 613-236 7391/92; fax: 613-236 6164; www.amba maroc.ca.

South Africa: Moroccan Embassy, 799 Schoeman Street, Arcadia, Pretoria 0083; tel: 012-344 2340; fax: 012-343 0613.

UK: Moroccan Embassy, 49 Queen's Gate Garden, London SW7 5NE; tel: 020-7581 5001/4; fax: 020-7225 3862.

US: Consulate General of Morocco, 10 East 40th Street, New York, NY 10016; tel: 212-758 2625; fax: 212-779 7441; www.moroccan consulate.com.

Moroccan Embassy, 1601 21st Street, NW, Washington DC 20009; tel: 202-462 7979; fax: 202-265 0161.

EMERGENCIES

The following numbers are useful 24 hours a day in an emergency:
Police 19
Fire 15
Brigade Touristique tel: 024-384601 (Tourist Police)
Ambulance tel: 024-443724
Polyclinique du Sud tel: 024-447999/7619, 24-hour emergency care (corner of rue de Yougoslavie and rue Ibn Aicha, Guéliz).

ETIQUETTE

Marrakesh is a cosmopolitan city, but Muslim women generally still keep their arms and legs covered (as well as their heads), so it is respectful to dress modestly, particularly when walking in the souks. The same rules apply when you are heading for the countryside, where the people are even more traditional.

Access to mosques and holy places in Marrakesh is restricted to Muslims, with the following exceptions: Medersa Ben Youssef *(see page 38)* and the mosque in Tin-Mal *(see page 72)*.

If you are invited to someone's home, take off your shoes before entering the room.

If you want to take a photograph of someone, particularly a woman, ask first as some may not like it. When you are eating, handle food with your right hand, as the left is for bathroom use. During Ramadan avoid eating or drinking in public when everyone else is fasting.

G

GAY AND LESBIAN TRAVELLERS

Gay sex is illegal under Moroccan law; the Moroccan penal code prohibits any sex act with a person of the same sex and allows for imprisonment of six months to three years plus a fine. In reality, however, due to sexual segregation in the Muslim culture, homosexuality is relatively widespread. Few Moroccans will admit to being gay: being the passive partner is taboo, and the dominant partner would not consider himself gay. Prosecution is very rare, unless it involves an under-age party. The concept of lesbianism is totally taboo in Morocco.

A fair amount of cruising does go on, however, in the Jemaa el-Fna after 11pm. Most nightclubs are gay-friendly, but there is more of a gay scene at the Diamant Noir (Hotel Marrakesh, avenue Mohammed V, Guéliz; tel: 024-434351), Beach Klubber (avenue Hassan II, opp Gendarmerie Royale, Guéliz; tel: 024-422877; www.beachklubber.com) and VIP (place de la Liberté; tel: 068-168999). Many *riads* are run by gay couples and actively attract gay couples to stay.

GETTING THERE (see also AIRPORT)

By air. Marrakesh's airport is linked by daily scheduled direct flights to most European cities. An increasing number of budget carriers now fly to Marrakesh. Royal Air Maroc (www.royalairmaroc.com) is Morocco's national airline. It has a 24-hour call centre (tel: 090-000800) for flight information, reconfirmation and reservations. Their office in Marrakesh is at 197 avenue Mohammed V Guéliz (tel: 024-425500). British Airways (www.britishairways.com) also has direct fights, as do the budget carriers Atlas Blue (www.atlas-blue.com), Easyjet (www.easyjet.com) and Ryanair (www.ryanair.com). There are a few direct flights from North America to Casablanca, but most flights go through a European city.

By rail. Trains are operated by the national railway company **ONCF** (tel: 024-447768; www.oncf.ma). Morocco has an excellent railway system, clean and efficient, and Marrakesh is the southernmost terminus of two lines, which go via Casablanca and Rabat: one to Tangier, and one to Oujda via Fez and Meknes. *(See also PUBLIC TRANSPORT, page 124).*

By bus. The bus station *(gare routière)* is at Bab Doukkala. *(See also PUBLIC TRANSPORT, page 124).*

By car. A good highway connects Marrakesh with Casablanca. There are good but rather slow roads to Essaouira and the coast, to Taroudant via the Tizi-n-Test, to Ouazarzate via the Tizi-n-Tichka and to Fez.

GUIDES AND TOURS

Tours. Information on tours is usually available from your hotel. **Marrakesh Tour Bus** (tel: 025-060006) is an open-top double decker bus with a running commentary in several languages, which follows two circular routes. Buses leave from place Abdelmoumen Ben Ali, opposite the Tourist Office, every 30 minutes for the first route from 9am–5pm and every 80 minutes from 9.50am–3.50pm for the second, but you can hop on or off where you like. The first route covers the sights in the city, the second does the Circuit de la Palmeraie. Tickets can be bought on board (Dh130) and are valid for 24 hours.

Guides. It is easy enough to find your way around the medina armed with a map or a guidebook, but a good guide will give more insight into the place. An official guide can be obtained through your hotel or through the Office National Marocain de Tourisme (ONMT; *see TOURIST INFORMATION, page 127*), for Dh150–200 for half a day.

H

HEALTH AND MEDICAL CARE

Morocco has good doctors *(médecins)* and most pharmacies have a good supply of drugs, but it can be hard to find someone who speaks English. Ask your hotel concierge for a doctor; or contact the **Polyclinique du Sud** (corner of rue ibn Aïcha and rue de Yougoslavie, Guéliz; tel: 024-447999) which has a 24-hour emergency medical and dental service; or **SOS Médecins** (tel: 024-404040) for an emergency call-out service (Dh450 per consultation). **Dr Bennani** is an English-speaking dentist at 112 avenue Mohammed V in Guéliz.

Most pharmacies are open Monday–Friday from 9am–noon and 3–7pm. Each pharmacy has a notice in the window giving the address of the *pharmacie de garde* – the pharmacy that is on duty until midnight or at weekends. The Pharmacie Menara (tel: 024-430415) on Jemaa el-Fna is open late, and the Polyclinique du Sud can provide emergency drugs after midnight.

The most common complaints suffered by visitors are upset stomachs and sunstroke. Don't drink tap water and avoid street food if you have a sensitive stomach; it's also wise to avoid undercooked meat, salads, fruit (unless you can peel it yourself) and dairy products as well as restaurants that look as if they have dubious hygiene. Bring plenty of rehydration salts, such as Dioralyte. Wear a sunhat and drink plenty of bottled water.

Make sure you have adequate travel insurance as Morocco has no reciprocal agreement with other countries to provide free medical care for visitors.

No compulsory immunisations are required to enter the country.

Where's the nearest (all night) pharmacy?	Où est la pharmacie (de nuit) la plus proche?
I need a doctor/ dentist	J'ai besoin d'un médecin/ un dentiste
an ambulance	une ambulance
hospital	un hôpital
I have an upset stomach	J'ai mal au ventre
sunburn/a fever	un coup de soleil/une fièvre

HOLIDAYS (Jours Fériés)

There are two kinds of holiday in Morocco: secular and religious. Banks, post offices, government offices and many other businesses will be closed on the following secular holidays:

Jan 1	New Year's Day
Jan 11	Independence Manifesto Day
May 1	Labour Day
July 30	Feast of the Throne
Aug 14	Oued Eddahab Allegiance Day
Aug 20	King and People's Revolution Day
Aug 21	King Mohammed VI's Birthday and Young People's Day
Nov 6	Anniversary of the Green March
Nov 18	Independence Day

Religious holidays. Muslim festivals follow the lunar Hegira calendar, a few days shorter than the Western solar calendar. **Fatih Muharram** is the Muslim New Year. Ten days later, the **Achoura** commemorates the assassination of Hussein, grandson of Mohammed. The **Aïd es-Seghir**, or **Aid el Fitr**, marks the end of Ramadan and most offices and shops are closed for two days. The **Aïd el-Kebir**, 70 days later, is a two-day holiday during which families slaughter a lamb to commemorate Abraham's willingness to sacrifice his son. **Aïd el-Mouloud** is the birthday of the Prophet Mohammed.

Do you speak English?	**Est-ce que vous parlez anglais?**
excuse me	**pardon**
you are welcome	**je vous en prie**
yes/no	**oui/non**
please	**s'il vous plaît (formal), s'il te plaît**
thank you	**merci**
where/when/how	**Où/quand/comment**
day/week/month/year	**jour/semaine/mois/année**
left/right	**gauche/droite**
near/far	**près/loin**
cheap/expensive	**bon marché/cher**
open/closed	**ouvert/fermé**
hot/cold	**chaud/froid**
old/new	**vieux/nouveau**
Please write it down.	**Est-ce que vous pouvez l'écrire?**
What does it mean?	**Qu'est-ce que cela veut dire?**
Help me please.	**Aidez-moi s'il vous plaît.**
Just a minute	**un moment**
What time is it?	**Il est quel heure?**

Sunday	**dimanche**
Monday	**lundi**
Tuesday	**mardi**
Wednesday	**mercredi**
Thursday	**jeudi**
Friday	**vendredi**
Saturday	**samedi**
What day is it today?	**Nous sommes quel jour aujourd'hui?**
today	**aujourd'hui**
yesterday	**hier**
tomorrow	**demain**

L

LANGUAGE

Most people in Marrakesh speak French and Moroccan Arabic, which differs from the Arabic spoken in the Middle East. Quite a large part also speaks Tashelhait or Chleuh, the local Berber language, and more and more people speak English. On the opposite page are some useful phrases to help you get by in French.

M

MAPS (plan de la ville)

The tourist office will give you a free map of Marrakesh, as will most hotels. More detailed maps are for sale at the bookshops *(see page 86).*

MEDIA (média)

The main European newspapers and the *International Herald Tribune* as well as many magazines are easily available in Marrakesh, usually 24 hours old. The best newsstands are on avenue Mohammed V in Guéliz, on the corner of rue de Mauritanie and next door to the tourist office. Most local magazines are in French or Arabic. For listings, check the monthly French-language free sheet *Couleurs Marrakesh Pocket* (www.marrakechpocket.com), available from more up-market restaurants and shops.

MONEY (Argent)

The local currency is the Moroccan dirham, abbreviated Dh or MAD. The dirham is divided into 100 centimes or francs. Coins of 5, 10, 20 and 50 centimes and of 1, 5 and 10 dirhams are in circulation, along with notes of 20, 50, 100 and 500 dirhams.

Everyone is always short of change, particularly taxi drivers, so hang on to yours if you can; it makes transactions easier.

Currency exchange. The easiest currency to carry is Euros, but British pounds sterling and US dollars are easily exchangeable at Moroccan banks. Normal banking hours are Monday–Friday 8.30–11.30am and 2.30–4.30pm.

Bureaux de change near the Jemaa el-Fna are open longer hours, and the Hotel Ali (rue Moulay Ismail) as well as other main hotels will exchange money at any time at a less favourable rate. Keep your receipt, as you can exchange excess dirhams into your own currency at the airport.

Credit cards, travellers' cheques and ATMs. International credit cards are widely accepted, although some smaller shops and restaurants will only accept cash. Travellers' cheques are accepted by most banks but stick to the better-known brands such as American Express and Thomas Cook. A commission is usually charged.

There are numerous cashpoints (ATMs, *distributeur automatique*) all over Marrakesh and Essaouira, but it is harder to find one out in the countryside. The exchange rate is better than for cash or travellers' cheques, but your bank will probably charge you for the withdrawal. Currently the withdrawal limit per day is Dh2,000. If you need more, take your card and passport to an exchange office or bank and take out a cash advance.

Can I pay with this credit card?	**Je peux payer avec une carte?**
I want to change some pounds/dollars.	**Je veux changer des livres anglais/dollars.**
Can you cash a traveler's check?	**Vous changez des chèques de voyage?**
Where is the bank/ currency exchange/ cash machine?	**Où se trouve la banque/ le bureau de change/ distributeur automatique?**
How much is it?	**C'est combien?**

O

OPENING HOURS

The working week is generally from Monday–Friday with a half day on Saturday, but some shops in the medina are open daily, while some close on Friday afternoon.

Banks. Monday–Friday 8.30–11.30am and 2.30–4.30pm.

Shops. Monday–Saturday 9am–1pm and 3–7pm.

Museums and sights. Opening times vary but most are closed on Tuesday.

P

POLICE (See also CRIME AND SAFETY and EMERGENCIES)

The main police station (Hôtel de Police) is on rue Oued el-Makhazine in Guéliz near Jnane Harti (emergency tel: 19), but any crime against a tourist should immediately be reported to the Brigade Touristique (Tourist Police), on the northern side of the Jemaa el-Fna (tel: 024-384601). The Gendarmerie Nationale is in control of the roads, and they frequently set up posts just outside the city to catch those speeding. Fines need to be paid on the spot.

| Where's the nearest police station? | **Où est le bureau de police le plus proche?** |
| I've lost my wallet/ bag/passport | **J'ai perdu ma portefeuille/ mon sac/mon passeport** |

POST OFFICE (Bureau de poste)

The main post office (PTT Centrale) is on place du 16 Novembre in Guéliz. It's open Monday–Saturday 8am–2pm. There is a branch on rue Moulay Ismail near the Jemaa el-Fna (Monday–Friday 8am–3pm). Stamps can also be bought at hotel reception desks or at a *tabac* (cigarettes stall). The mail service is very slow, so if your mail is urgent, use the express service (EMS) or an international courier service.

Where's the post office?	**Où est la poste?**
express (special delivery)	**expresse**
a stamp	**une timbre**
air mail	**par avion**

PUBLIC TRANSPORT

Local buses. There are few local buses in Marrakesh. Most of those that do exist operate between the city centre and the suburbs to take local people between home and work, and are not really useful to visitors. Bus number 1 leaves from the place de Foucault near the Jemaa el-Fna and goes to Guéliz along the avenue Mohammed V. Buses 3 and 8 run from the same square to the train station on avenue Hassan II.

Taxis. The best way of getting around town is by taxi, although these do not exactly constitute public transport. The *petit taxi* can take a maximum of three passengers, cannot leave city limits and charges by the meter so make sure it is switched on. Expect to pay 50 percent more from 8pm onwards. A taxi from the Jemaa el-Fna to Guéliz costs about Dh10. The *grands taxi is* inexpensive and takes up to six passengers. There are no fixed departure times; the taxi departs when all the seats are full. You simply turn up at the 'terminal' (the tourist office or your hotel will tell you where this is; it is often next to the main bus station).

Intercity buses. The bus station *(gare routière)* is at Bab Doukkala, outside the medina walls. There are long-distance buses to most Moroccan cities operated by CTM (tel: 024-433933; www.ctm.co.ma) or the superior Supratours (tel: 024-435525), who run the fastest bus to Essaouira (Dh75; 3½ hours). Except on these express services, which have air-conditioning and videos, bus travel over long distances can be uncomfortable. If you have a choice, it is better to take the train.

Train. Trains are operated by the national railway company **ONCF** (tel: 024-447768; www.oncf.ma). The railway station is on avenue Hassan II, Guéliz, but a new one is under construction right next to it facing avenue Mohammed VI and is due to open at the end of 2008. As the southernmost terminal, Marrakesh has regular connections with Casablanca, Rabat, Tangier, Oujda, Fez and Meknes.

Buses 3 and 8 go from the station to the Jemaa el-Fna, and a line of *petits taxis* waits outside the station – a journey should cost from Dh10–20. There are no trains further south or to Essaouira.

Where can I get a taxi?	**Où est-ce que je peux trouver un taxi?**
What's the fare to ...?	**C'est combien pour le billet de...?**
Where is the bus stop?	**Où est l'arrêt de bus?**
When's the next bus to ...?	**Le prochain bus pour.... part quand?**
A ticket to ... single/return	**Un billet pour... Aller/aller retour**
Will you tell me when to get off?	**Est-ce que vous pourriez me dire où je dois descendre?**

R

RELIGION

Morocco is a Muslim country, but is tolerant of other religions. Christians account for about 1 percent of the population. Most Moroccans belong to the Sunni branch of Islam. Muslims pray five times a day in the direction of Mecca (Saudi Arabia), and go to the mosque particularly for the Friday midday prayer. Most mosques and religious buildings are closed to non-Muslims. Muslims fast between the hours of sunrise and sunset during the holy month of Ramadan, and during this month visitors should eat and drink discreetly during the day. The tourist office can provide a list of religious services for English-speaking Roman Catholic visitors, but there is no Anglican church in the city.

T

TELEPHONE

Morocco's international code is **212**, the code for Marrakesh is **024**, and this area code needs to be dialled even within the region. To call abroad from Morocco dial first 00 then the country code (44 for UK, 1 for the US), followed by the phone number.

Telephone calls can be made from phone boxes *(cabines)* on the street or in a main post ofice. They take Dh1 and Dh5 coins or phone cards; the latter are available from *tabacs*, news vendors or phone shops. It is best to use a phone card for international calls. Private pay-phone booths *(téléboutiques)* are widespread; clean and efficient, they cost little more than a pay phone on the street.

TIME ZONES

Morocco follows Greenwich Mean Time (GMT) all year round. It is on the same time as Britain in winter, but an hour behind during British Summer Time.

TIPPING

In cafés and restaurants a tip *(pourboire)* of 10–15 percent of the total bill should be given. Everybody else who peforms a service for you will expect a small tip of about Dh10–20. This includes attendants *(gardiens)* at monuments and museums as well as porters and parking attendants.

TOILETS

There are very few public toilets in Morocco, so always use the facilities in a hotel or restaurant if possible. Carry some toilet paper as it is not always available.

| Where are the toilets? | **Où sont les toilettes?** |

TOURIST INFORMATION

The main tourist office in Marrakesh is on place Abdelmoumen, Guéliz (tel. 024-436131). The office is open Monday–Friday 8.30am–4.30pm, and Saturday morning.

Moroccan Tourist Offices (ONMT; Office National Marocain de Tourisme; www.visitmorocco.com) are maintained in several countries including the following:

Australia: 11 West St, North Sydney, NSW 2060; tel: 02-9922 4999.
Canada: PI Montéal Trust, 1800 Rue McGill College, Suite 2450, Montreal, PQ H3A 2A6; tel: 514-842 8111.
UK: 205 Regent Street, London W1R 7DE; tel: 020-7437 0073.
US: 20E 46th Street, Suite 1201, New York NY 10017; tel: 212-557 2520; PO Box 2263, Lake Buena Vista, Orlando, FL 38230; tel: 407-827 5335.

WEBSITES

The most useful websites are:
www.visitmorocco.com The official website of the Moroccan tourist office.
www.ilove-marrakesh.com Best website on Marrakesh's history, festivals, weather, hotels, restaurants, *hammams*, galleries and nightlife.
www.morocco.com Includes hotel bookings and travel tips.

Recommended Hotels

A *riad* is a traditional house in the medina, with rooms set around an internal garden or courtyard. Many have been bought by foreigners who spend their holidays here, or who run them as a *maison d'hôte* or guest house. New *riads* seem to open every week in Marrakesh – there are now more than 600 registered bed-and-breakfasts in the medina alone, and a lot more unregistered ones. *Riads* are often very attractive, and come in all price brackets, but most fit into the mid-range and expensive categories.

Staying in a *riad* offers a chance to experience living in a typical Moroccan house, or indulging in a designer's dream, but many visitors start to feel a little claustrophobic after two or three days. After staying a few days in the medina many prefer to move to a hotel with more space and a pool in Hivernage, the Palmeraie or out of town in Essaouira. Christmas and New Year, Easter and spring are counted as high season, while at other times of the year many hotels offer a low season tariff.

The rates given here are for a double room and include taxes and breakfast.

$$$$$	over Dh2,000
$$$$	Dh1,300–2,000
$$$	Dh750–1,300
$$	Dh300–750
$	under Dh300

JEMAA EL-FNA AND AROUND

Gallia $$ *30 rue de la Recette, tel: 024-445913, fax: 024-444853, www.ilove-marrakesh.com/hotelgallia.* Delightful family-run *pension* in a quiet backwater very close to the Jemaa el-Fna. There are 17 cosy, spotlessly clean rooms, situated off two tranquil courtyards with a fountain and a turtle, where a delicious breakfast is served under the trees. Great views can be had from the terrace and there is a solarium too. The staff are friendly and welcoming, with an old-style Marrakesh flair. Book ahead, as it fills up quickly.

Grand Tazi $ *corner of avenue el-Mouahidine and rue Bab Agnaou, tel: 024-442787, fax: 024-442152.* Old-style Marrakchi hotel with slightly faded but comfortable and clean rooms, bang next to the Jemaa el-Fna. Popular with budget tour groups, there is a good-sized pool, a restaurant that cannot be recommended and a lively bar that sells the cheapest beer in the area.

Hotel de Foucauld $ *avenue el-Mouahidine, tel: 024-440806.* Another old-timer, popular with those who knew the city before the *riad* explosion, as well as with tour groups who head off for the mountains soon after breakfast. The rooms are spacious, if a bit dark, and from the rooftop terrace you can pick up the buzz of the nearby Jemaa el-Fna.

Jnane Mogador $ *1116 Riad Zitoun el-Kedim, tel: 024-426324, www.jnanemogador.com.* This small charming *riad* with 17 clean, comfortable rooms, offers very good value for money and therefore fills up quickly, so book ahead. The terrace gives fabulous views of the medina and the Atlas Mountains. The staff are friendly enough, but can be a bit quirky. No heating in winter.

Riad de l'Orientale $$ *8 Derb Ahmar, Quartier Laksour, tel/fax: 024-426642, mobile: 061-142103, www.riadorientale.com.* Small family-run *riad* in a 250-year old house with comfortable rooms. A far cry from designer boutique hotels, the British owners have kept the traditional Moroccan style and offer a warm welcome. Wi-fi access throughout.

Riad Lotus Ambre $$$$–$$$$$ *22 Fhal Zefriti Bab Laksour, tel: 024-411405, www.riadslotus.com.* One of several luxurious Lotus *riads*, all with over-the-top contemporary decor and the latest technology including Bang and Olufsen plasma screens and sound systems.

Riad Yima $$–$$$ *52 Derb Arjane, Rahba Kedima, tel: 024-391987, www.riadyima.com.* Small hotel designed by London-based Moroccan pop art artist Hassan Hajjaj, with great colourful rooms and very friendly service. There is a small boutique where you can buy the artist's art and designs.

Sherazade $$ *3 Derb Djamaa, Riad Zitoun el-Kedim, tel: 024-429305, www.hotelsherazade.com.* Large *riad*-style hotel with pleasant rooms set around peaceful large tiled courtyards. All this together with friendly, welcoming staff make it a popular option if the Gallia is full.

NORTHERN MEDINA

Dar Attajmil $$$ *23 rue Laksour, off rue Sidi el-Yamami, tel: 024-426966, www.darattajmil.com.* Right in the middle of the chic Mouassine area, this four-room *riad* is a little oasis. Very welcoming and stylishly decorated with Italian good taste. The rooms overlook a courtyard with banana trees and palms, and the roof terrace is bliss.

Maison Arabe $$$$ *1 Derb Assebhe, Bab Doukkala, tel: 024-387010, www.lamaisonarabe.com.* Once a famous French restaurant, this became the medina's first *maison d'hôte* in 1998. This is old-style Marrakchi opulence, with luxurious rooms decorated in a blend of Moroccan and colonial style and set around two lush courtyards. The hotel has a good smart restaurant and a renowned cookery school.

Nejma Lounge $$–$$$ *45 Derb Sidi M'hamed el-Haj, Bab Doukkala, tel: 024-382341/071-518957, www.riad-nejmalounge. com.* Small *riad* with six rooms, decorated in pop-art style and colours. This is a young and funky place, with a relaxed atmosphere, smallish but extremely comfortable rooms, a plunge pool and a great rooftop terrace.

Noir d'Ivoire $$$$$ *32 Derb Jdid, Bab Doukkala, tel: 024-381653, fax: 024-381653, www.noir-d-ivoire.com.* A large *riad* named after the darkest shade of black, with large sumptuous rooms decorated in earthy tones with contemporary African accessories. There is a delightful courtyard restaurant and an interesting trendy Moroccan fashion boutique.

Riad el-Fenn $$$$$ *2 Derb Moulay Abdallah ben Hezzian, Bab el-Ksour, tel: 024-441210, www.riadelfenn.com.* Contemporary

Moroccan crafts are mixed with some great Brit-art works at this *riad* belonging to Vanessa Branson (sister of Richard). Three houses have been brought together, and everything is light, spacious, uncluttered and tranquil. Grand bar and a lovely restaurant serving locally sourced food.

Riad Farnatchi $$$$$ *2 Derb el-Farnatchi, Qa'at Benahid, tel: 024-384910, www.riadfarnatchi.com.* Five houses in the heart of the medina were first transformed by the British hotelier Jonathan Wix into a holiday house for himself and friends. It was too good to be left empty most of the year, so it is now a sumptuous and intimate hotel, run by the fabulous Lynn Perez who can arrange anything and knows the whole of Marrakesh.

Riad Tarabel $$$$ *8 Derb Sraghna, Dar el-Bacha, tel: 024-391706, www.riadtarabel.com.* One of the newcomers, the Tarabel offers a zen-like experience with elegant rooms in toned-down colours, decorated with family heirlooms such as huge paintings and old mirrors – all set around a simple green courtyard. Breakfast is served on the grand rooftop terrace.

Riyad Edward $$$–$$$$ *10 Derb Marestane, Zaouia Abbasia, Bab Taghzoute, tel: 024-389797/061-252328, www.riyadedward. com.* You can see why this house has been the backdrop for so many fashion shoots. The rambling old palace is full of period detail, decorated with gorgeous tiles, lots of finds from the nearby junk market and books everywhere. It feels more like a friend's home than a hotel.

Tchai'kana $$$ *25 Derb el-Ferrane, Azbest, tel: 024-284587, www. tchaikana.com.* With subtle white and light interiors softened by some sub-Saharan textiles, this is a chic and laid-back hotel with just four large rooms around a splendid courtyard. The place is run smoothly by a welcoming young Belgian couple who love to share their love of Marrakesh with their clients.

Tlaata wa-Sitteen $$ *63 Derb el-Ferrane, Riad Laarous, tel: 024-383026, www.tlaatawasitteen.com.* Offers excellent value in neat, simple and comfortable rooms. Proprietors Kamaal, his brother Saeed and Najjat welcome their guests like long-lost friends, and every night somehow turns into a gathering. This is old-style Marrakesh, and Najjat's cooking is strongly recommended.

SOUTHERN MEDINA

Angsana Riads $$$$$ *rue Riad Zitoun el-Jdid, tel: 024-421979, fax: 024-421372, www.angsana.com.* The Angsana-Banyan Tree is the first international hotel chain to move into the medina. They run six beautiful *riads* just off rue Riad Zitoun el-Jdid in the southern medina (same contact details for all of them). All have spas, for which the company is famous, and each has its own individual atmosphere and decor. The restaurants serve Asian fusion cuisine.

Dar Fakir $$$ *16 Derb Abou el-Fadal, off Riad Zitoun el-Jedid, tel: 024-441100, www.darfakir.com.* Callling itself the *riad* for the clubbing generation, this is owned by the city's hippest restaurateur Nourdine Fakir, who started Villa Rosa *(see page 140)* and Nikki Beach *(see page 90).* Lots of cushions, candles, incense and Buddha Bar music makes the whole place feel like a chilled lounge club, and the rooms are extremely comfortable.

Hotel du Trésor $$ *77 Sidi Boulokat, off Riad Zitoun el-Kedim, tel: 024-375113, www.hotel-du-tresor.com.* Totally delightful little hotel, open in the 1950s, and now owned by an Italian, who kept the traditional courtyard and tiles but added some funky objects, mostly from other historic hotels in the town. The rooms are set around a quiet courtyard with a magnificent orange tree and small pool. Recommended.

Riad Kaiss $$$$ *65 Derb Jedid, off Riad Zitoun el-Kedim, tel: 024-440141, www.riadkaiss.com.* Another stunning *riad* renovated and owned by French architect Christian Ferré, who kept the Moroccan style of the house while adding a contemporary architectural touch. The result is eye-catching and calming, with beautiful earth-coloured spaces and a cool dip pool.

Riad Kasbah $$$ *101 Derb Harbil, Kasbah; tel: 024-387405, www.riadkasbah.com.* Perfectly located near the Saadian Tombs, this small guesthouse, with 10 rooms and suites around a dip pool and large courtyard, is decorated in muted colours but also has many touches of the warm reds and yellows of Marrakesh. Guests can use the private traditional indoor *hammam*.

Riad W $$$ *41 Derb Boutouil, Kennaria, tel: 065-367936, www.riadw.com.* Funky *riad* with four rooms and spacious living areas, decorated in a simple neutral colour palette, 1970s furniture and contemporary furnishings. The simplicity is welcome after the sometimes overwhelming assault on the senses in the souks.

Sultana $$$$$ *rue de la Kasbah, Kasbah, tel: 024-388088, www.lasultanamarrakech.com.* The Sultana looks old but it's completely new. This boutique hotel and spa, decorated in opulent style, offers all the luxury you could hope for. The staff outnumber the rooms, the spa is renowned and the pool is a good size to swim in.

GUÉLIZ AND HIVERNAGE

El-Saadi Hotel and Resort $$$$–$$$$$ *avenue el-Qadissia, tel: 024-448811, www.essaadi.com.* This *grande dame* of old Marrakesh hotels still oozes charm and has a great mature garden and a large pool. The newly opened resort extension has an opulent feel, but the service is not entirely up to standard yet.

Hotel du Pacha $–$$ *33 rue de la Liberté, tel: 024-431327, fax: 024-431326.* Crying out for a revamp, this hotel is run-down but full of atmosphere. Bedrooms are comfortable and have clean en suite bathrooms; some rooms have balconies.

Hotel Toulousain $ *44 rue Tariq ibn Ziad, tel: 024-430033, www.geocities.com/hotel_toulousain.* This long-established budget hotel, where beat writer William Burroughs and his friends used to hang out, is still going strong with basic but clean rooms in the heart of the new town.

PALMERAIE

Les Deux Tours $$$$$ *Douar Abiad, tel: 024-329525, www.lesdeuxtours.com.* A plush garden hotel in the Palmeraie, with a good pool and *hammam*. A favourite among fashion photographers, and more affordable than some of the private villas nearby.

Jnane Tamsna $$$$$ *Douar Abiad, tel: 024-329423, www.jnanetamsna.com.* A haven in the Palmeraie on the edge of Marrakesh, these five beautiful villas are decorated by owner Meryanne Loum-Martin and set in a splendid perfumed garden created by her husband, ethno-botanist Gary Martin. Most of the food comes from the organic garden, each villa has its own pool, and the rooms are the latest in African-Middle Eastern chic. Cooking classes, yoga, reflexology, massage and tennis coaching are all on offer.

Palais Rhoul $$$$$ *Km5, Dar Tounisi, Route de Fes, tel: 024-329494, www.palaisrhoul.com.* Formerly a family residence, the Palais Rhoul has a sense of Roman opulence with grand, spacious rooms, a salon with a circular pool that seemingly escaped from a James Bond movie and some seriously luxurious *caidal* tents that allow guests to live the Oriental fantasy to the full. Even if this is beyond your budget, pay a visit to try one of the best *hammams* in Morocco.

OURIKA AND HIGH ATLAS

Kasbah Bab Ourika $$$$$ *Ourika Valley, tel: 061-252328/024-420248, http://babourika.com.* This new hotel is majestically perched on a hilltop in the lush Ourika Valley with 360-degree panoramic views over traditional Berber villages, the Atlas Mountains and the lush river valley below. It offers beautiful rooms and the chance to relax in the gardens where there's a pool, or to trek in the gorgeous surroundings.

Kasbah du Toubkal $$–$$$$$ *Imlil, Asni (60km/38 miles from Marrakesh), tel: 024-485611, fax: 024-485636, www.kasbahdutoubkal.com.* The Kasbah du Toubkal, situated at the foot of Jbel

Toubkal, the highest peak in North Africa, is an extraordinary hotel run by a Brit together with local Berbers. The home of a local ruler was transformed into a range of accommodation from a comfortable mountain refuge to luxury suites with incredible views. The Kasbah is so much more than a hotel: it is a place of meditation for those seeking total total peace and quiet. The hotel runs a lodge further into the mountains so you can walk between the two.

CASCADES D'OUZOUD

Riad Cascades d'Ouzoud $$ *in Ouzoud, tel: 023-459658, www.ouzoud.com.* Perched on top of the waterfalls, this friendly and very welcoming guesthouse has nine bedrooms decorated in rustic chic with local textiles and furnishings. The owners also run treks in the surrounding countryside, and breakfast on the roof terrace is truly spectacular.

ESSAOUIRA

Dar Beida $$$$ *tel: 067-965386, www.castlesinthesand.com.* Gorgeous 18th-century medina house decorated by London designers Emma and Graham. Organic forms and shapes in the traditional architecture are painted in white lacquer, and the rooms are furnished with cool iconic furniture dating from the 1950s and 1960s; some found in junk markets in Morocco, others brought here from their store in London. The house is bathed in light and has a great rooftop terrace.

Hotel Beau Rivage $–$$ *145 place Moulay Hassan, tel/fax: 024-475925, www.essaouiranet.com/beaurivage.* A recently refurbished long-established budget hotel with views over the most popular square in town, clean rooms with spotless private bathrooms, and a great rooftop terrace that overlooks the port and town.

Madada $$$-$$$$ *5 rue Youssef el-Fassi, tel: 024-475512, www.madada.com.* Small guesthouse with just six very stylish and comfortable rooms, some around the roof terrace with sweeping views over the beach, the harbour and the Bay of Essaouira.

Recommended Restaurants

Eating in Marrakesh can be delicious and cheap if you eat on the Jemaa el-Fna or wildly expensive in some of the trendy places in town. Some of the restaurants in the medina offer only a set menu of several courses of Moroccan food, accompanied by music, at a fixed price.

The cheaper restaurants are open throughout the day, while most others open for lunch from noon–3pm, and again for dinner from 7.30 or 8pm to 11pm. Most places need to be booked in advance.

The rates given here are for a three-course meal and include taxes and service, but not drinks.

$$$$$	over Dh4,500
$$$$	Dh3,000–4,500
$$$	Dh1,500–3,000
$$	Dh750–1,500
$	under Dh750

JEMAA EL-FNA AND AROUND

Argana $–$$ *Jemaa el-Fna, tel: 024-445350.* Daily 6am–11pm. No alcohol. This is a huge no-nonsense café-restaurant overlooking the square, with cheap Moroccan dishes and a perfect view, especially at dusk.

Café de France $ *Jemaa el-Fna.* Daily 6am–11pm. No alcohol. This once famous café is not what it used to be, but still a good place for a mint tea away from the crowds, with great views over the city and Atlas Mountains from the rooftop.

Café des Epices $ *75 Rahba Kedima, tel: 024-391770.* Daily 8am–8pm. No alcohol. A great place to hang out on the lively square of the Rakhba Kedima. You can seek the shade inside or enjoy the views from the roof terrace, listen to cool music or chat with the young Moroccans who run the place. A perfect lunch spot with Wi-fi, mint tea, snacks, sandwiches and salads.

Chez Chegrouni $–$$ *Jemaa el-Fna, tel: 065-474615*. Daily 6am–11pm. No alcohol. Favourite old-timer in the square that still serves cheap no-frills couscous, *tagines* and Moroccan salads at reasonable prices.

Le Marrakchi $$$ *52 rue des Banques Jemaa el-Fna, tel: 024-443377, www.lemarrakchi.com*. Daily 11.30am–11pm. If it's your first time in Marrakesh then this is the place to start. The Marrakchi has great views over the square, romantic decor on the second floor, and decent Moroccan food without too many spices. Unusually for restaurants on the square there is also a wine list.

Terrasses de l'Alhambra $$ *Jemaa el-Fna*. Daily 8am–11pm. No alcohol. A café-terrace, more elegant than most, serving a good espresso, ice cream and a menu of light snacks and salads. The terrace is a favourite meeting place, but on a hot day there is the attraction of air-conditioning inside.

Le Tobsil $$$$ *22 Derb Abdellah ben Hussayn, Bab Ksour, tel: 024-444052*. Wed–Mon 7.30–11pm. One of the best medina palaces, serving an elaborate Moroccan set menu in spectacular surroundings with a good evening show of traditional music.

NORTHERN MEDINA

Dar Chérifa (Café Littéraire) $$ *8 Derb Charfa Lakbir, tel: 024-426463, www.marrakech-riads.net*. Daily 9am–7pm. No alcohol. This beautifully restored 16th-century house with elegant carved beams and fine stucco work has been turned into a literary café and art gallery. A perfect place to relax after shopping with a light lunch.

Dar Moha $$$$ *81 rue Dar el-Basha, tel: 024-386400, www.darmoha.ma*. Tue–Sun for lunch and dinner. Great setting in a French villa with a swimming pool in the garden. Moha Fedal made his name and fame cooking traditional Moroccan dishes with a fusion twist. The food, part of a choice set menu, looks and tastes excellent, but the service can be hit and miss. Reservations essential.

Dar Yaqout $$$$ *79 rue Ahmed Soussi, Arset Ihiri, tel: 024-382929.*
Tue–Sun for dinner only. Dar Yaqout is set in an opulently decorated palace, designed by Bill Willis. They serve a set menu, and it's quite a spectacle. Guests are led through the house, lit by 1,001 candles, before being served a true banquet. Book ahead and don't eat for days before you come.

Le Foundouk $$$$ *55 rue du Souk des Fassi, Kat Bennahid, tel: 024-378190, www.foundouk.com.* Tue–Sun noon–4pm and 7pm–midnight. Wildly stylish restaurant on several floors with a great roof terrace. Serves an attractive French-Moroccan menu.

Le Pavillion $$$$ *Derb Zaouia, Bab Doukkala, tel: 024-387040.* Wed–Mon dinner only. Sit under the giant tree outside or in the small intimate salons inside for one of the more up-market eating experiences in Marrakesh. The menu, mainly French with a few local flavours, is written on a blackboard, and the food, served in beautiful surroundings, is excellent.

Terrace des Epices $$ *15 Souk Cherifia, Sidi Abdelaziz, tel: 024-375904/076-046767.* Daily 10am–midnight. Delightful new venture from the team that owns the Café des Epices *(see page 136)*, with a simple but gorgeous, vibrant terrace offering shaded booths, Wi-fi and cool lounge music. The menu is equally simple but delicious – keep some space for the prunes with fresh goat's cheese for dessert.

SOUTHERN MEDINA

Kosybar $$$ *47 Place des Ferblantiers, tel: 024-380324.* Tue–Sun noon–11pm. The Kosybar is a popular meeting place for a sundowner or late-night drink, but there is also food available, ranging from Moroccan-Mediterranean dishes to Japanese prepared by the sushi chef. The owner is the son of a Moroccan vineyard owner, so the impressive wine list comes as no shock. At weekends there is live music in the piano bar.

Le Tanjia $$$$ *14 Derb Jdid, tel: 024-383836, http://letanjia. blog.com.* Daily 10am–1am. Oriental brasserie on the edge of the

Jewish Mellah with sumptuous contemporary Moroccan decor, palm trees and elegant Moroccan cuisine. Waterpipes and tea on the terrace in the afternoon.

Café du Livre $$ *44 rue Tarek ibn Ziyad, tel: 024-432149.* Mon–Sat 9.30am–9pm. Sandra Zwollo's café-cum-bookshop has become a favourite hangout for anglophiles. The bookshop has an excellent selection on its shelves and the shop and the adjoining café-restaurant both have Wi-fi access. Excellent breakfast served until 11.30am. The delicious lunch is Mediterranean-style and there is a wonderful selection of cakes in the afternoon.

Café Les Négociants $ *place Abdelmoumen, avenue Mohammed V, tel: 024-435782.* Daily 6am–11pm. Parisian-style café-terrace that serves a good breakfast and a light lunch, but mostly this is a place to meet friends and have a coffee.

Catanzaro $$$ *42 rue Tarek ibn Ziyad, tel: 024-433731.* Mon–Sat for lunch and dinner. This Italian-French restaurant becomes more popular by the year, and the quality is consistent. It can be relied on for excellent pizzas and grills, swift service and good desserts. There are now three sittings an evening and it is advisable to book ahead; as prices are good value it is popular with local families as well as tourists.

El-Fassia $$$–$$$$ *Résidence Tayeb, 55 boulevard Zerktouni, tel: 024-434060.* Daily for lunch and dinner. This wonderful Moroccan restaurant, the best in town, is run by an all-women's cooperative. They serve a wider selection of classic Moroccan food than most. Specials like *mechoui* (roast lamb) need to be ordered 24 hours in advance. Reservations are essential.

Grand Café de la Poste $$$–$$$$ *corner of boulevard Mansour ed-Dahbi and avenue Imam Malik, tel: 024-433731, www.grand cafedelaposte.com.* Daily 8am–1am. This is *the* place in town to see and be seen. The grand colonial-style terrace buzzes with *le tout*

Marrakesh, particularly at night. It's a great place for a drink, albeit an expensive one, and the simple fusion menu is consistently good. A great one for people-watching.

Kechmara $$$ *3 rue de la Liberté, tel: 024-422532, www.kechmara.ma.* Mon–Sat 7am–midnight. This is a popular laid-back restaurant, furnished in 1960s style, and serving a small menu of delicious light Mediterranean food. There's a great rooftop terrace for an alfresco lunch in spring and summer.

Lolo Quoi $$$$ *82 avenue Hassan II, tel: 072-569864.* Daily 7.30pm–midnight. Busy Italian-Mediterranean restaurant serving Italian classics with a modern twist. The decor is contemporary and so is the music, attracting the expat crowd.

Niagara $$ *32 Centre en-Nakhil, Route de Targa, tel: 024- 449775.* Tue–Sun noon–2.30pm and 7.15–11pm. Cheap and cheerful pizzeria with red and white gingham tablecloths and a wide variety of good thin-crust pizzas baked in a wood-fired oven. Very popular with local families.

Oliveri $ *9 boulevard Mansour ed-Dahbi, tel: 024-448913.* Daily 10am–11pm. A Marrakesh institution, this old-fashioned ice cream parlour is still one of the best in town. Take away a cone or have one of the huge selections of *coupes*. Not easy to find as it is in a side street off the boulevard, but everyone knows it.

Villa Rosa $$$$$ *64 avenue Hassan II, Guéliz, tel: 024-449635.* Daily for dinner only. Trendy venue run by the city's hippest restaurateur, Nourdine Fakir. There's a covered terrace with slender bamboo and an elegant interior furnished with plush red velvet and lit by numerous candles. Simple French dishes with a twist, deliciously prepared and beautifully presented.

HIVERNAGE

Alizia $$$ *corner of rue Ahmed Chawki and avenue Ech-Chouhada, tel: 024-438360.* Daily for lunch and dinner. Old-fashioned

Italian-Mediterranean restaurant popular with the older expat crowd. The food is excellent: great pizzas and a large selection of well-prepared fish dishes as well as a few local specialities like *tanjia*, a stew prepared in pottery vessels. This is a great place to lunch or dine alfresco in the garden.

Le Comptoir $$$$$ *avenue Ech-Chouhada, tel: 024-437702*. Daily 4pm–1am, until 2am at weekends. The food here can be fine but tends to be unpredictable. People really come to this talked-about restaurant-cum-bar-cum-boutique-cum-nightclub for the guaranteed party atmosphere, particularly when the belly dancers arrive every night at 10.30pm.

Crystal $$$$$ *Pacha Club, Boulevard Mohammed VI, Zone Hôtelière, Agdal, tel: 024-388480, www.pachamarrakech.com*. Daily for lunch and dinner. Within the Pacha nightclub compound, this elegant restaurant is run by the Michelin-starred Pourcel twins. The menu is inventive Mediterranean with slight Italian overtones, using the best local produce mainly from the Ourika Valley. The restaurant has a pool so this makes a fun lunch option with a swim, and the atmosphere at the weekends is great.

Table du Marché $ *corner of rue du Temple and avenue Ech-Chouhada, tel: 024-421212*. Daily 7am–11pm. Excellent patisserie and tearoom that serves fine French tarts and croissants as well as delicious sandwiches.

La Villa $$$$ *avenue Kennedy, tel: 024-421969*. Tue–Sat for lunch and dinner, dinner only Mon. Gastronomic French restaurant that has built up a good reputation for affordable, excellent and beautifully presented food since its opening in 2006. There is alfresco dining in summer.

AROUND MARRAKESH

La Pause $$$$ *Douar Lmih Laroussième, Agafay, tel: 061-306494, www.lapause-marrakech.com*. Daily for lunch and dinner. La Pause offers a Moroccan lunch or dinner with views of the desert, a relaxing time away from the buzz of Marrakesh, and opportunity to camel ride, hike or see a spectacular sunset over the desert.

Chalet de la Plage $$ *1 boulevard Mohammed V, tel: 024-479000.* Daily for lunch and dinner. With a terrace right on the sea, this is the place for no-nonsense fresh fish and seafood accompanied by a glass of chilled white wine.

Chez Sam $$$$ *Port de Pêche, tel: 024-476238.* Daily for lunch and dinner. At the very end of the harbour stands this wooden shack in the shape of a ship decorated in nautical style, with aquariums, fishnets and portholes. This is a legendary restaurant where Sam, a jazz musician, used to entertain his musical friends and feed them delicious seafood. These days the jazz is gone and the food is average, but it's hard to beat a plate of fresh oysters with a glass of chilled white wine while watching the fishing boats come in.

Elizir $$–$$$ *1 rue d'Agadir, tel: 024-472103, www.elizir.com.* Daily for dinner. Abdellatif must be the most charming restaurateur in the country, and his restaurant is the kind of place you would choose to go every night once you have discovered it. The setting is a traditional Moroccan townhouse but furnished with 1960s and 1970s pieces Abdellatif found in local junk markets. The Moroccan-Italian menu changes, but is always delicious and inventive, with dishes such as delicious *tagines* of all kinds, homemade ravioli with fresh goat's cheese, and steak with black chocolate sauce. The little tapas that arrive at your table are on the house, as is mint tea.

Taros $$–$$$ *place Moulay Hassan, tel: 024-476407, www.taros cafe.com.* Mon–Sat 11am–4pm and 6pm–midnight. The Taros rooftop bar sits atop a tall house overlooking the harbour and main square. This is the place for a sundowner or a cocktail later in the evening, while the seagulls perform their aerial ballet. On the first floor there is a salon with a large library of books about Morocco, a boutique and a good restaurant.

INDEX

Berlitz pocket guide

Marrakesh

First Edition 2008
Reprinted 2011

Written by Sylvie Franquet
Edited by Pam Barrett
Series Editor: Tom Stainer

Photography credits
Alamy 47, 60, 63, 72, 91; Corbis 70; Mary Evans
19; Getty 15; Tony Halliday 10; Alan Keohane
77; Clay Perry 6, 9, 12, 13, 17, 22, 24, 27, 28, 30,
31, 32, 34, 39, 40, 43, 44, 45, 46, 48, 51, 52, 53,
55, 56, 57, 59, 62, 67, 68, 71, 74, 75, 78, 79, 80,
82, 83, 84, 87, 89, 92, 93, 95, 96, 99, 101, 102,
103; Topfoto 21; Phil Wood 37

Cover picture: Alex Armitage/Robert Harding

Every effort has been made to provide
accurate information in this publication,
but changes are inevitable. The publisher
cannot be responsible for any resulting
loss, inconvenience or injury.

Contact us

At Berlitz we strive to keep our guides as
accurate and up to date as possible, but if you
find anything that has changed, or if you have
any suggestions on ways to improve this guide,
then we would be delighted to hear from you.

Berlitz Publishing, PO Box 7910,
London SE1 1WE, England.
email: berlitz@apaguide.co.uk
www.berlitzpublishing.com